AF481140

DR. ANNEPAUL VEMAGIRI

The Trainer's Compass

Navigating the Path to Effective Training

Contents

Thank you

"We all need a compass in our life journey, and I am fortunate to have more than one."

To my Mummy and Daddy, thank you for guiding me every single day since the very beginning of life's journey.

To my sister Usha, who has been like a parent to me, standing by my side throughout my entire journey, thank you for your unwavering love and strength.

To my brother Vinay, who has always been ahead of me, showing me the way, along with Rachel and Patrick, thank you for being my guiding lights.

And to the compass of my writing journey, Heena—this book is a reality because of you. Thank you for being my support, my cheerleader, the believer of my work and words, and for guiding me to bring this book to life.

Purpose

This book aims to provide a comprehensive guide for you if you are a trainer, a coach, or a writer, blending personal stories, practical training techniques, and insights into effective learning and teaching methodologies. It is designed to inspire and equip you with the tools you need to excel in your role.

On February 24, 2025, my three books were released, published, and ordered. Now, my mind is settled to begin my fourth book. I had a chat with Heena, and as usual, we brainstormed around the book title, which we both agreed upon. I had many drafts created over the last three years, and my mind couldn't settle on anything. However, one thing I was sure about was that I wanted to write about training or learning and development—my profession, something that I'm passionate about.

"Training is neither my job nor my career; it is not my profession or my calling. It is what it is—a passion deeply rooted, the very love of my life."

When I was thinking about my profession, I wondered if it was my choice or if I was meant to do it. Did I choose learning and development, or did learning and development choose me? This made my head spin. It took me a lot of time to settle down. I felt discomfort thinking about when I started, where I started, and why I started being a trainer. I always believe one doesn't need inspiration for what they're meant to do in life, and I'm 100% sure I was never inspired by anybody. So if you ask me who was my inspiration to be a great trainer, I wouldn't be able to answer that question. I wasn't inspired to be a trainer; I wasn't asked to be a trainer; I wasn't even pushed into this profession. I did not choose this profession; it has been a part of my life.

So, I'm standing at this point in my life and career, looking back at the years I've spent teaching people and simplifying information. With years of experience in delivering training to so many learners—the number I do not remember—I want to write a book that serves as a simplified guide or compass for trainers. It ensures that you, as a trainer, do your job in the most effective and efficient manner.

Here I am, writing down in a different manner, which you will further read as you open the book and read each chapter. What I have done for you is that I have picked up eight parts. Each part has chapters based on each number; for example, eight has eight chapters. The idea is to make the book interesting to navigate. I personally wanted to have clarity in my mind because I like to work around interesting formats. I had a lot of content around training—around 28 years of it. This is what I have only done, so I wanted to come up with something definitely different and unique, yet very simple.

In this book, I have added very simple language and graphics for you. Instead of reading the text, you just look at the graphic and understand. I've added simple examples, my stories in between, and a lot of space for you to find your own way to be the trainer you are. My book will become a compass for you to navigate towards your passion, profession, and calling, or, as I say, your love of your life.

Overview

This book aims to provide a comprehensive guide for trainers, coaches, and writers, blending personal stories, practical training techniques, and insights into effective learning and teaching methodologies. It is designed to inspire and equip you with the tools you need to excel in your role.

It has 8 Parts as below:

One Story: My Story

1. Every trainer has a unique journey, and this chapter shares mine—from my early days as a curious learner to my evolution into a seasoned trainer. This narrative sets the stage for the lessons and insights ahead.

Two Sides of a Trainer

1. Learning: The Receiving Aspect (Yin) of a Trainer
2. Training: The Giving Aspect (Yang) of a Trainer

Three Hats of a Trainer

1. The Trainer: Discover how the "TRAINER" within emerges to inspire and educate.
2. The Coach: Explore how the "COACH" surfaces, guiding others on their paths.
3. The Writer: Witness how the "WRITER" breathes creativity into the training process.

Four Walls of a Trainer

1. Blank Wall: The feeling of hitting a creative or motivational block.
2. Perfect Wall: Crafting the ideal environment for impactful training sessions.
3. No Wall: Moving away from having zero motivation to

being self motivated.

4. Overflowing Wall: Managing information overload for a smoother, effective learning experience.

Five Senses a Trainer Can Activate

1. Visual: Utilizing visuals like slides or videos to enrich the learning journey.
2. Voice: Harnessing vocal techniques for clarity, engagement, and motivation.
3. Touch: Engaging learners with tactile, hands-on activities for practical learning.
4. Taste: Adding creative elements with memorable sensory experiences.
5. Smell: Using scents to create a stimulating and welcoming atmosphere.

Six NLP Brands

1. Belief Change: Techniques to help transform limiting beliefs into empowering ones.
2. Reframing: Shifting perspectives to view challenges and opportunities differently.
3. Anchoring: Associating cues with specific emotions or actions for impactful learning.
4. Neuro-Associative Conditioning: Combining conditioning with neural connections for growth.
5. Dissociation: Encouraging detachment from negative experiences to foster healing.

6. Swish Pattern: A behavior-change method to inspire positive actions effectively.

Seven Habits of Effective Trainers

1. Be Proactive: Take initiative and adapt to learners' needs.
2. Begin with the End in Mind: Set clear goals to guide learning outcomes.
3. Put First Things First: Prioritize tasks for impactful training.
4. Think Win-Win: Promote mutual success in the learning process.
5. Seek First to Understand, Then to Be Understood: Listen empathetically for better communication.
6. Synergize: Collaborate to achieve exceptional results.
7. Sharpen the Saw: Emphasize personal growth, self-care, and lifelong learning.

Eight Wastes in Training

1. Transportation: Streamline processes for efficiency.
2. Inventory: Manage materials to avoid waste or shortages.
3. Motion: Optimize movements for ergonomic practices.
4. Waiting: Minimize downtime to improve productivity.
5. Overproduction: Balance content to avoid overwhelming learners.
6. Overprocessing: Simplify training for better focus and understanding.
7. Defects: Ensure quality by addressing and reducing

errors.

8. Skills: Continuously refine and enhance your expertise
   as a trainer.

Sum to Someone

At 36, I found myself in the valley of life, surrounded by doubt and fear. Psalm 23:4 became my guiding light: "Even though I walk through the darkest valley, I will fear no evil, for you are with me." Repeating these words, I gradually rediscovered my strength. Step by step, I rose from the shadows, climbing toward the mountain top—a place of triumph and renewed faith.

The number 36 holds deep significance in my life. It marks the age when I restarted my journey, investing in new learnings and personal growth. Now, as I look back from the mountain top, I see the valley I once stood in. But instead of despair, I see beauty—I see myself as the lily of the valley, resilient and blossoming.

Embark on a transformative journey of personal growth and discovery. This book takes you through a path that widens with every step, from one to eight, revealing the clarity and depth of the love of our life—Learning & Development. Each chapter illuminates a milestone in this journey, leading you towards your purpose and a flourishing sense of being a trainer.

Achieving

THE SUM

12345678

Training – Learning & Development

Training is like sculpting marble into a masterpiece—each chip and polish represents the refinement of skills, the honing of knowledge, and the shaping of attitudes. With purpose as the sculptor's vision, the learner emerges transformed, equipped to excel in their craft or field.

Understanding Training

Simply put, training is the art of turning complexity into clarity—streamlining data to nurture skills, broaden knowledge, and shape attitudes. It is a purposeful endeavor aimed at enhancing the learner's capability in specific areas, whether for tasks, professional growth, or personal development.

Let's adapt the definition of a trainer to the role of a waiter and examine the three criteria that elevate her or him to a true performer. I am using the example of a waiter as it is more relatable to my field of expertise that is hospitality. You may have your own example from your own industry.

1. Attitude and Behavior

A neat and professional appearance conveys attention to detail and creates a positive first impression. This includes wearing a clean uniform, being well-groomed, and maintaining hygiene standards. Good posture, such as standing straight and walking confidently, exudes professionalism and composure. It also helps with physical stamina during long shifts. A friendly smile, a polite tone, and maintaining eye contact can make guests feel welcome and valued. Being approachable encourages guests to ask for assistance without hesitation.

2. Skills

This involves the step-by-step sequence to follow seamlessly and effortlessly for the task to serve the guest while anticipating guest needs and making sure the service is on a timely basis.

3. Knowledge

A performer-level waiter knows the menu inside out, including ingredients, preparation methods, and potential allergens. This allows them to provide accurate and thoughtful recommendations. Whether it's suggesting wine pairings, explaining a dish's flavour profile, or discussing dietary accommodations, being well-prepared to respond to guest queries.

The Outcome

When a waiter combines these aspects, they don't just meet expectations—they exceed them. They transform a meal into a memorable experience where guests feel genuinely cared for. This builds customer loyalty and leads to glowing reviews and recommendations, creating a win-win for both the individual waiter and the establishment.

Apply the definition of Training to any job role relatable to you

Job Role

Attitude

Skill

Knowledge

Outcome

THE TRAINER

If training is like sculpting, then a trainer is the sculptor—patient, skilled, and visionary. Just as a sculptor shapes raw marble into a masterpiece, a trainer refines the potential of learners, chiselling away doubts, polishing skills, and crafting confidence. They bring out the beauty and strength within, one deliberate stroke at a time.

The trainer, the chiseller and the sculptor also have two sides to his or her personality. Just like a coin has its value when both sides are present. Similarly, a trainer has two sides: to train and to learn when the trainer has these both sides, the trainer carries highest value

Also, to train others, a trainer requires attitude, skill, and knowledge to develop the mind of a learner in an efficient and effective manner.

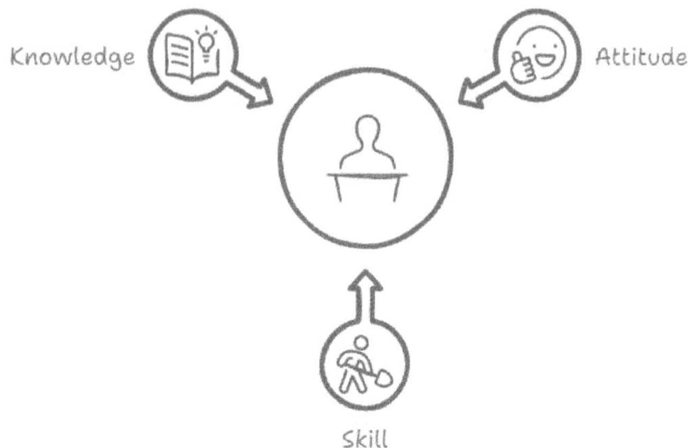

On the part of a trainer, it requires clarity in your own mind as a trainer. Once you have that clarity, imparting information to someone else becomes easier. Training, as I see it, is one-way directed: the trainer passes information to the learner. The learner depends on the trainer and looks up to them, literally with their head looking up in a classroom, eyes fixed on the trainer who imparts information with utmost clarity.

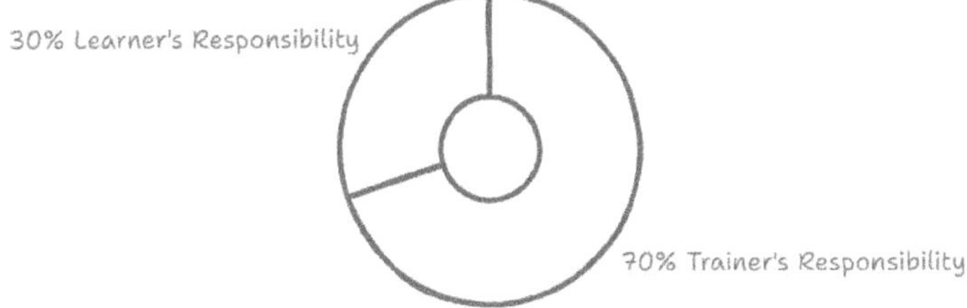

In training, 70% of the responsibility lies with the trainer and 30% with the learner. However, 100% results are expected from the learner. Therefore, the trainer must be well-prepared. My benchmark is always 100. To reach that 100, the trainer must work backward and delve deeply into the clarity of the topic to be taught. The trainee or learner is totally dependent on the trainer's knowledge, skill, and behavior, which I call attitude. The trainer is always in control, even though it may seem like the control is given to the learner. The control switch remains with the trainer.

Training is a very effective form of learning and development, especially in classroom settings or groups of learners who are either starting out or have been pushed to be in that space for their own development. It's an excellent way to bring a group of people to a state of learning and growth. This is one of my favorite methods when addressing a large number of people. The results are amazing and depend entirely on the trainer, who must be well-prepared to simplify and present the vast amount of information available in the world in a fun and engaging manner.

I know this from experience, as it took me a lot of hard work to keep improving myself as a trainer. In the early days of my career, I struggled to remember information. I used to make tiny bits of paper and stick them in my tutor's journal to remind myself in case I missed any information. At times, I made errors and let go of incorrect information. I went back to my learners, accepted my fault, and replaced the wrong information with the correct one. It took a lot of courage, but it helped. That's when I decided that a lot of work needed to be done on my own skills as a trainer. Over time, I realized that the more I worked on my knowledge, the more it grew. Knowledge is unlimited, so I decided to focus on what I could control: my attitude and behavior as a trainer. I chose to be positive, vulnerable, honest, and carry integrity in my training while enjoying what I do.

Secondly, I decided to sharpen my skills as a trainer through practice. Since then, I have never let down any opportunity to train any number of people on any topic or any kind of learner. I found every opportunity to conduct trainings, whether in a classroom, online, or one-on-one. I took pride and pleasure in conducting trainings because this way, I was sharpening my own skills. Over time, I realized this is the only way a trainer can be effective. I started training, teaching, and lecturing in all forms that I could, and this became my sharpest tool that I carry even today. A trainer's skill must be sharpened every day. Never miss a day, moment, hour, or minute to find an opportunity to train someone who is ready to look up to you, right into your eyes, seeking clarity.

Training for me involves a lot of hard work on the trainer's part, and it equally adds up to their behavior or attitude, skill, and knowledge. When a trainer is well-balanced in these three elements, the information becomes simple, and learners enjoy being around such trainers. They look for trainers who make information simple and fun. Learners remember such trainers and often compliment them. I still receive compliments that I have been one of the best trainers they have come across, and it definitely motivates and boosts me to continue doing what I do so well.

LEARNING

Learning, by definition, involves acquiring attitude, skill, and knowledge. As I progressed in my career as a trainer, I came across a new term: learning. Many hotels started renaming their training managers as learning managers or learning and development managers. This raised the question: what is the difference between these two professions from the same fraternity? Do they perform their jobs differently? What was expected of me as a learning manager or learning and development manager?

I did some introspection and research, and the best approach was to examine both words and find the difference. As per my understanding, training is one-way, while learning is two-way. In training, the trainer has higher accountability, whereas in learning, the accountability lies more with the learner. If training involves 70% accountability of the trainer and 30% of the learner, then in learning, 70% lies with the learner and

30% with the trainer.

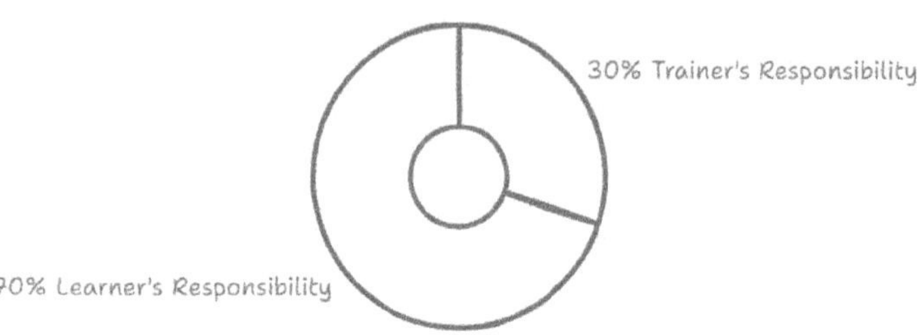

I started developing this mindset through discussions with leaders around me and the changing times. I realized that I was putting in a lot of hard work and effort to simplify information for someone who needed to learn or develop, which was justifiable because that was my duty. I assumed it was my 100% duty to do so. However, when the concept of learning came into focus, I started to question whether it was really my sole obligation or if it was the learner's accountability.

When I asked this question, the answer I received was that it is not solely on me; it is significantly the learner's role to take ownership of their learning. I concluded that while I would continue to simplify and present information in the best possible manner, if the learner is not ready, motivated, or inspired to learn, then as a trainer, I can only do so much.

However, if the motivation comes from the learner, meaning the learner takes full accountability, then this creates a better equation.

Learning, for me, is where the efforts are equally shared by the trainer and the learner. It is more like a relationship, a partnership where both the trainer and the learner work together to elevate their knowledge, skill, or behavior to the next level for their development.

LEARNING & DEVELOPMENT

Imagine that you are the gardener, and your mind or skills are the soil. Seeds represent knowledge, ideas, and experiences you encounter. Initially, you plant these seeds with intention—choosing the ones you want to grow. But planting isn't enough. You must nurture the soil by watering it with curiosity, feeding it with the nutrients of practice and reflection, and giving it sunlight through exposure to new perspectives and challenges.

And just like a garden takes time, patience, and consistent care, so does personal and professional development. Over time, those seeds bloom into vibrant plants, fruits, and flowers—a flourishing representation of your expanded capabilities and understanding.

And that's what Learning & Development is—it is the deliberate act of planting, nurturing, and transforming seeds of potential into a flourishing mind that is ready to learn and grow. The gardener, who is the trainer, isn't just a caretaker; a trainer is a creator, an architect of the landscape of the mind, cultivating the fruits of growth and development.

Choti and Dr. Annepaul Vemagiri

Bridging Time: A Conversation Between My Younger Self and Me

Reflection is such a powerful tool for growth, and I've found a unique way to engage with it. I've started having conversations between my younger self, Choti, and the present-day me, Dr. Annepaul Vemagiri. Through these dialogues, I create a space where curiosity meets experience, and exploration merges with understanding.

Meeting Choti

Choti is my younger self, eager, full of questions, and brimming with dreams. She's in that phase of life where the world feels vast and endless, yet slightly overwhelming. Every step she takes feels like a choice that could shape her future. And now, here I am, stepping into the picture as her older self, someone who has walked this path, faced the unknowns, and gathered lessons along the way.

The Conversation Begins

Choti comes to me with her questions—simple yet profound. Questions like:

- "How will I know if I'm making the right choices?"
- "What if I fail at my dreams?"
- "What truly matters in life?"

As I respond, I'm careful not to impose but to guide. I want her to discover, to think, and to embrace life with all its uncertainties. What I share is not just advice but a perspective—a perspective shaped by time, experience, and reflection. And in answering her, I find myself revisiting the same questions, reflecting again on their answers in light of who I am today.

Why This Matters

Engaging in these dialogues is more than just a reflective exercise. It's a journey that bridges the gap between the person I was and the person I've become. It allows me to honour Choti's journey, her dreams, and her struggles while also acknowledging my growth. Together, we navigate the past and the present, learning from each other in unexpected ways.

Through these conversations, I've come to realize that my younger self isn't just a memory—she's a part of men and by speaking with her, I'm nurturing the seeds she planted, ensuring they continue to bloom.

A Perspective for the Perspective

This practice is deeply personal, but it has universal appeal. It's about connecting with who we once were, understanding our journey, and shaping our path forward. By bringing Choti and

Dr. Annepaul Vemagiri together, I've created a dynamic where the wisdom of experience meets the enthusiasm of youth, and together, we craft a narrative that celebrates both.

And perhaps, in these conversations, there's something for everyone to take away—a reminder that our past selves hold the questions that can still shape our present and future.

I

One Story

Every trainer has a unique journey. In this chapter, I share my personal story, from my early days as a learner to becoming a seasoned trainer. This narrative sets the stage for the lessons and insights that follow.

The Differences that made the Difference

Every story has two sides; for clarity, one must get to know both sides of the same part.

The First Difference

As a kid, I used to collect old class notebooks, write questions in them, and then also write answers and make corrections. I think I loved the tick sign. Then I would give scores, which were never the same. They were random. My tiny fingers never worried about their size but were always focused on the size of excitement they used to have and then acted accordingly.

Today, I know that's when my trainer journey started. I used to be fascinated by the corrections my teachers made in our notebooks. The signature authority to signify that 'all is well'. It was more about practicing control on paper, and I just loved the process of it. Although none of these realizations were clear to me back then, now, when I look back, I find myself always looking forward to the power of Tick or Cross – the first difference.

The Second Difference

This fire within me took me to become and serve as a Sunday School teacher for 12 years, teaching kids aged 6 and 7 the Bible stories every Sunday. The whole thing was natural to me and needed no extra effort to start, but then I wanted to stop somewhere after 12 years, as I felt that even my Sundays were not for me anymore. So it took me a lot of effort to stop – teaching during weekdays and teaching on a Sunday – the second difference.

The Third Difference

Fast forward into adulthood; this was when I was working as a Training Manager in one of the prestigious hotels in South India. As part of my career growth, it was always recommended that we move from the training department to human resources. When I looked back at my own education, I realized that I had completed my master's in business administration in human resources and also a postgraduate diploma in the same field. So, when this thought was shared with me, I wanted to change. I wanted to move. I wanted something different to happen to me. I said yes, I want to be the Human Resource Manager because, again, this was giving me power. I wanted to learn new things and explore this new area in my life. I was so proud and so happy, and I was celebrating. But when I started taking up the responsibility, I felt my mind was totally clogged. I couldn't feel myself. I used to drag myself out of bed. It was definitely not comfortable. I was treading in a space where I was so uncomfortable. I felt powerless. What made me feel powerless? This is the question I asked myself day in and day out. It felt like my spirit was residing in a different body. It wasn't my body that was weak , but my spirit, as if it were trapped inside a casket that wasn't mine at work

1.5 years of dragging myself each day. I did some good work as HR manager. I took some strong decisions, pushed my boundaries into the spa as a support and drove people's engagement. I handled a lot of colleagues' engagement programs and was also managing during the times when Chennai was flooded. But inside me, Anne was losing power. Anne felt helpless. Then I decided I needed to get powerful again. I needed to come back to where I belonged. I spoke to a lot of people, searched my heart, thought a lot, and then I said I'm going back to where I started my journey, and that's training. Working as Human Resources Manager or Training Manager – the third difference.

The Fourth Difference

This was in the year 2016, and I moved to a new job, a new country, and a new system of work. Right when you think you know it all is when you get to know that there is a new door, and it feels unknown.

This new workplace was quite dynamic and held many learnings for me to unfold. I was sitting in a session with a trainer who was a few years more experienced than me, and he opened a slide on the screen. It read, "Group Activity", and below it was a question in bold letters, "What is the difference between Coaching and Training?" Being a trainer for many years now, I assumed that this would be an easy task. We were asked to divide ourselves into two groups, and each group was to list five things we knew about each topic, i.e., Coaching & Training. I was in the group discussing Coaching. To my surprise, I couldn't think of anything. I sat there with my right thumb clicking the ballpoint pen and my left palm holding my jaw in surprise. I looked around for some clarity and then sat back in my chair, knowing that my knowledge was limited. Our trainer stopped us, signalling that time was up and it was time to discuss.

My learning ears were eager to know the difference. The trainer asked us to share one group at a time. The first group shared their list and their answers for Training: Training is to impart knowledge, Training is to help people grow, Training is improving skill & knowledge, Training is two-way, and Training is a skill. Our trainer was polite and appreciated the points.

Now, it was our turn to share, and I hid my face behind everyone as being the one who knew the least. One of us started putting forth her points and said that Coaching is asking questions and Coaching is listening to others. Our trainer appreciated our effort in sharing our discussion and also understood that we needed a little more dive into the two diverse and dynamic topics whose meanings are usually interchanged. Our trainer clapped her hands twice to call for our attention. As we gazed at her, she took an empty glass and kept it right in front of us. She then took a bottle of water and started pouring water slowly and mindfully, ensuring the water took time to fill the glass. She then took the filled glass and started drinking out of it, quenching her thirst as she wiped her mouth with the back of her palm. We were all wondering what had just happened. Then she said, "Pouring water into the glass is like Training, and drinking out of that glass filled with water to quench a person's thirst is Coaching." "Training fills us, and Coaching empties," she continued. "Training gives us all the nutrition that we want, and Coaching makes us use those nutrients for our growth," she concluded. Training and Coaching – the fourth difference.

These differences led me to find a balance in my life and clarity in my thoughts. Since then, I have been pursuing my passion as a calling and haven't turned around until today to pause and write what I have learned all these years in the chapters to come.

tête-à-tête

"I learnt that being a good trainer isn't about perfection. It's about connection—understanding people, listening to them, and sharing what you know in a way that makes sense to them."

Choti: *Dr. Annepaul, I always see you helping people learn and grow. Were you always this wise and amazing, or did you have to learn how to be a trainer?*

Dr. Annepaul: (smiling) Oh, Choti, that's sweet of you to say. But no, I wasn't always a trainer. My journey was full of twists and turns—each step teaching me something new. Would you like to hear about it?

Choti: Yes ! Tell me everything. Did it start when you were my age?

Dr. Annepaul: Hmm, you could say it started when I was your age. I was a curious child, just like you—always asking questions, eager to learn. But I wasn't the best student. I struggled with some subjects and didn't always feel confident. That's when I realized how important good teachers are.

Choti: Like someone who believes in you and helps you, right?

Dr. Annepaul: Exactly! I had a teacher who didn't just teach me facts but showed me how to think and believe in myself. That sparked my first thought: one day, I want to do that for others.

Choti: Wow! So you knew you'd be a trainer when you grew up?

Dr. Annepaul: Not exactly. I had to figure it out step by step. After school, I explored different jobs—some I loved, and some... not so much. But each experience taught me something important. I realized that I loved working with people, sharing ideas, and seeing them grow.

Choti: That's so cool! But wasn't it hard to become a trainer?

Dr. Annepaul: Oh, it was. I made mistakes, Choti—lots of them. In my early days, I tried too hard to be perfect. But then I learnt that being a good trainer isn't about perfection. It's about connection— understanding people, listening to them, and sharing what you know in a way that makes sense to them.

Choti: So you learnt from your mistakes too?

Dr. Annepaul: Every mistake was a lesson in disguise. Over time, I became more confident and adaptable. I also learnt that a good trainer is always a learner first. Even now, I learn from the people I train, just as they learn from me.

Choti: That's like Yin and Yang, right? Giving and receiving knowledge!

Dr. Annepaul: (beaming) Exactly, Choti! My journey as a trainer is really a balance—between sharing and growing, teaching and learning. It's been an adventure, and every step has shaped who I am today.

Choti: I think your story is amazing, Dr. Annepaul. Maybe I'll have my own journey one day, like you!

Dr. Annepaul: I'm sure you will, Choti. And no matter where your journey takes you, just remember—you have the power to make a difference, one step at a time.

II

Two Sides of a Trainer

The iconic concept of balance and duality in Chinese philosophy! Yin and Yang represent complementary forces that interact to form a dynamic system where the whole is greater than the sum of its parts. Together, they symbolize harmony and the interconnectedness of opposites within a person. The following two chapters explore how applying the Yin and Yang principle to a single trainer—who both gives and receives knowledge—reveals a fascinating harmony within the same individual.

THE RECEIVER

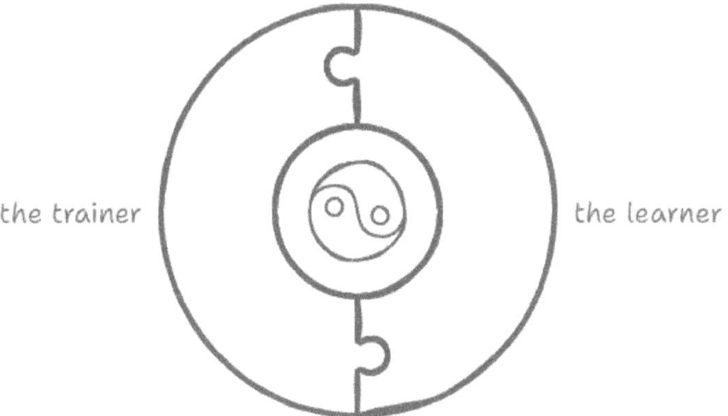

I n Chinese philosophy, "Yang" is one of the two fundamental aspects of the universe, paired with "Yin". Together, they represent the concept of dualism, where opposite or complementary forces exist in harmony and balance.

Yang embodies qualities like light, activity, warmth and expansion. It's associated with the sun, brightness, and energy that moves outward. In contrast, Yin represents calmness, coolness and contraction.

The Receiving Aspect (Yin)

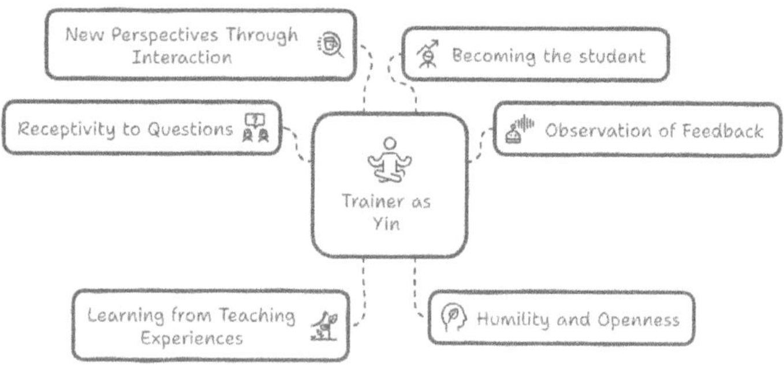

"Yin" is the complementary counterpart to "Yang" in Chinese philosophy. While Yang represents light, activity, and expansion, Yin embodies rest and contraction. It's associated with qualities such as coolness, passivity, receptivity, femininity, and inward energy. Yin is connected to the moon, shadows, and the nurturing aspects of life.

The interplay of Yin and Yang symbolizes the balance and harmony present in the universe. Neither is superior—they rely on each other to create wholeness.

In the same sense, the Trainer embodies Yin when they are receptive—listening to questions, observing feedback, and learning from their own teaching experiences. Every interaction with trainees offers new perspectives, insights, and lessons, making the Trainer a perpetual student.

Become a student or a learner. The more you embody this side of the coin, the more you will grow as a trainer on the outside. As Yin, the Trainer becomes a student and listens actively and attentively. This is a moment of learning—not just about the subject matter but about how others perceive and interpret it.

RECEPTIVE

Feedback is crucial for any Trainer, and the Yin aspect allows them to embrace it constructively. When the trainer transforms into a learner mode, they become the receiver of knowledge and feedback. Here we learn about being receptive.

REFLECTIVE

Yin encourages reflection, pushing the Trainer to view every learning moment as an opportunity for self-growth. It's a reminder that teaching is as much about learning as it is about guiding others.

REALISTIC

The Yin quality keeps the Trainer grounded and real. It

reminds them that knowledge is vast and evolving, and no one—no matter how experienced—has mastered everything. This humility fosters a stronger urge to continue to learn & grow.

RESPONSIBLE

A trainer becoming a learner understands the perspective of their students. These perspectives enrich the trainer's understanding and make them more adaptable and empathetic, making them respect and accept perspectives, making them a responsible professional.

RATIONAL

When the trainer operates in Yin mode, they become a perpetual student, understanding the truth that the trainer must constantly learn and evolve. This growth is not just professional but also personal, shaping them into a more effective and holistic individual.

Through this Yin aspect, the trainer becomes more than a teacher; they become a learner, a listener, and an observer. It's this interplay of giving and receiving that makes the teaching experience truly balanced and impactful.

What are your top 5 YIN qualities as a trainer ?

THE GIVER

The Giving Aspect (Yang)

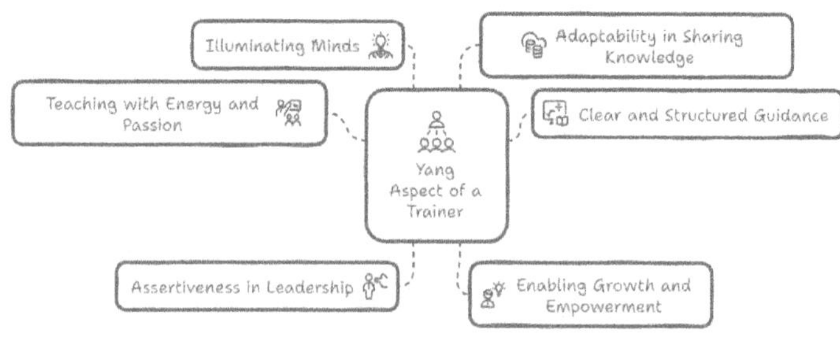

When the Trainer is sharing their knowledge, they are in the role of Yang. They actively teach, explain, and guide. This side thrives on assertiveness, clarity, and structure. It's the light they bring to illuminate their learners' understanding.

When a Trainer embodies the Yang aspect of imparting knowledge, they assume the role of an active leader, utilizing their expertise and energy to enlighten others.

Teaching with Energy and Passion

The Trainer's Yang quality shines through their ability to engage and inspire their audience. Their energy acts as a spark, igniting curiosity and motivation in their trainees. This vitality keeps the learning process dynamic and engaging.

Clear and Structured Guidance

A Trainer operating in the Yang mode ensures that their teachings are well-organized and accessible. They use logical frameworks, examples, and clear communication to simplify complex concepts, making them easier for the learners to grasp. This clarity is the "light" that cuts through confusion.

Assertiveness in Leadership

Yang is about confidence and decisiveness. The Trainer confidently steers the learning process, setting goals, expectations, and boundaries. Their assertiveness ensures that the trainees remain on track and focused, facilitating an effective learning environment.

Enabling Growth and Empowerment

As a giver of knowledge, the Trainer empowers others to grow. They nurture independence in their trainees, encouraging them to think critically, solve problems, and ultimately apply what they've learned in real-world scenarios.

Illuminating Minds

Symbolically, the Trainer becomes a beacon of light, illuminating new pathways of thought and opening doors to possibilities that were previously unknown to the learners. This enlightening role helps trainees not just accumulate knowledge but also see the bigger picture.

Adaptability in Sharing Knowledge

While Yang represents action and giving, a good Trainer tailors their teaching style to the needs of their trainees. They remain flexible in how they share knowledge, ensuring that it resonates with different individuals and learning styles.

Through their Yang qualities, the Trainer becomes a guiding force—a source of wisdom and understanding—helping their trainees navigate the learning journey with confidence and clarity. It's a role that carries great responsibility, as they are shaping the minds and potential of those they teach.

What are your top 5 YANG qualities as a trainer ?

tête-à-tête

**It's about balancing different parts of ourselves.
For a trainer, Yin could be the quiet
side—listening, learning, and reflecting. And
Yang could be the active side—teaching,
speaking, and guiding others. Together, they
create harmony.**

Choti: *Dr. Annepaul, I saw this cool symbol with a swirly black and white circle. Someone said it's called Yin and Yang. What does it mean?*

Dr. Annepaul: Ah, that's a beautiful symbol, Choti! Yin and Yang represent balance and harmony—like day and night, or hot and cold. They show how opposites work together to make a whole. One can't exist without the other.

Choti: Oh, like how I need both summer and winter to enjoy the seasons! But how does this work for people?

Dr. Annepaul: Great example! For people, it's about balancing different parts of ourselves. For a trainer, Yin could be the quiet side—listening, learning, and reflecting. And Yang could be the active side—teaching, speaking, and guiding others. Together, they create harmony.

Choti: So a trainer has to do both—like teaching and learning at the same time?

Dr. Annepaul: Exactly! For example, when a trainer teaches, they're in their Yang energy—sharing knowledge. But when they listen to participants' questions or adapt to their needs, they're using their Yin energy. It's a dance between the two.

Choti: That's so cool! But what happens if someone has too much Yang or too much Yin?

Dr. Annepaul: That's a great question, Choti. If a trainer focuses only on Yang—teaching and speaking—they might not connect with their participants. If they focus only on Yin—listening and reflecting—they might not share their knowledge effectively. Balance is key.

Choti: So they have to be like that swirly circle—both black and white together?

Dr. Annepaul: You've got it! And here's something fun: the Yin and Yang symbol also shows that a little bit of one exists in the other. Even when a trainer is teaching, they can still learn from their students. And even when they're listening, they can share insights.

Choti: Whoa, it's like being two things at the same time! Can I try being Yin and Yang too?

Dr. Annepaul: Of course, Choti! Think about times when you're quiet and thoughtful—that's your Yin. And when you're full of energy, talking or creating—that's your Yang. Balancing both helps you grow and connect with others.

Choti: I like that! I'm going to practice being both. Thanks, Dr. Annepaul—you're like my wise Yin-Yang trainer!

Dr. Annepaul: (smiling) And you're my curious little philosopher. Keep exploring these ideas, Choti. You've got a natural balance already!

III

Three sides (Coach - Trainer - Writer)

As I began my journey as a trainer, I noticed two shadows working alongside me. When I let the sun go down, these shadows became a part of me. Each day, as I started to focus more, they emerged as two individual personalities from within me. When I looked around, I saw the same thing happening to others.

The next three chapters take you through defining each personality, and they complement each other in the trinity of becoming the unique Learning & Development professional you aim to be.

THE TRAINER

I nteresting trio! "Coach," "trainer," and "writer" represent distinct yet overlapping roles that share a common thread of inspiring and guiding others.

Over time, in my transition from a lost soul to finding my being, I reached a point when I found my calling, which is to train others. As I dived deeper inside me, I found more to it. There was a coach within me. I concluded I have two callings, but then time took a turn, and I went deeper within to find the writer in me.

Trainer

Specialises in teaching specific skills or knowledge, often in a more structured or technical way, such as fitness training, corporate training, or skill-building workshops.

Coach

Focuses on helping individuals or teams improve and achieve goals, often emphasizing mindset and strategy. Coaches may work in sports, business, or personal development.

Writer

Creates content—be it storytelling, documentation, or educational material. Writers engage minds and emotions, shaping ideas through words.

Here how a being a coach, trainer, and writer interconnects and complement one another using

SHINE

STORYTELLING

Coaches often use stories to inspire, trainers utilize examples to explain concepts, and writers create narratives to engage. Storytelling is a powerful tool that unites these roles.

HUMAN CONNECT

All three roles require the ability to communicate effectively. A coach motivates and strategizes, a trainer imparts knowledge and skills, and a writer crafts messages or narratives. At their core, they share the need to connect ideas with people.

IMPACT

Whether improving performance (coach), building skills (trainer), or sparking ideas (writer), all these roles aim to create a positive and lasting impact.

NORTH POLE

Coaches and trainers guide others toward achieving their goals, while writers inspire, inform, or provoke thought through their words. Each role influences growth and understanding, though the medium and approach may differ to lead the learner to their North Pole, which is their individual purpose.

EMPATHY

A coach must understand the mindset of their team, a trainer needs to gauge their audience's learning style, and a writer should resonate with their readers. Empathy is key to excelling in all three.

In fact, one person could embody all three roles seamlessly. For example, someone could write about personal growth (writer), conduct workshops on it (trainer), and work one-on-one with clients to overcome challenges (coach).

The "trainer in a trainer" is the essence of teaching and skill-building—a dedication to nurturing growth, improving abilities, and empowering individuals to reach their full potential.

Here's how the "TRAINER" emerges within a trainer

T - TRAINED

A trainer prioritizes self-growth, understanding that effective training begins with their own continuous learning and self-improvement.

R – RAPPORT BUILDING QUALITY

The trainer fosters meaningful connections, creating an atmosphere where learners feel valued, motivated, and excited to engage.

A - AGILE

A trainer learns about each learner individually and changes himself or herself as per the learner, becoming more agile to people and data.

I – INSPIRATIONAL

A trainer sparks enthusiasm and confidence, encouraging learners to pursue their goals with passion and determination.

N - NURTURING

By cultivating growth, a trainer ensures that learners feel supported, valued, and empowered to succeed.

E - EMPOWERING

Beyond teaching, an exceptional trainer builds confidence in learners, encouraging them to apply their newfound skills with independence.

R - REFINING

A trainer is improves continuously enhancing their methods to guide learners towards excellence.

THE COACH

A coach is someone who guides and supports individuals or teams to achieve their goals, improve their performance, and develop their skills. Coaches can work in various fields, such as sports, business, personal development, and education. Their role often involves providing feedback, setting goals, creating strategies, and motivating their clients or team members.

Ah, the coach within a trainer! This speaks to the deeper, more personal aspect of training—the ability to inspire and empower people beyond just teaching skills.

Here's how the "COACH" emerges within a trainer

C – CONSISTENT

A coach consistently inspires individuals to push beyond their limits, believe in their potential, and stay dedicated to their goals.

O – OBJECTIVE-FOCUSED

A coach emphasizes a clear, larger vision for success—guiding trainees to align their efforts with long-term personal or professional aspirations.

A - AGILE AND ADJUSTABLE

Coaching embraces flexibility, tailoring strategies to individual needs. A coach-trainer hybrid understands that no two learners are the same and adjusts approaches accordingly.

C – CONFIDENCE BUILDER

More than just imparting skills, a coach instills unwavering self-belief, nurturing confidence that extends far beyond the training environment.

H – HOW & WHY gap filler

A coach fosters a deeper understanding, helping trainees not only master the "how" but also connect with the "why." For example, a fitness trainer with a coaching mindset might link workouts to a broader wellness journey.

This blend of coaching and training creates a transformative experience, enabling the trainee to gain knowledge while feeling empowered, guided, and inspired to grow.

THE WRITER

A writer is not just the one who generates content in written form, but also the one who has a powerful idea and also the powerful way to mould that idea into books, articles or social media content. Here the writer owns the responsibility of spreading the ideas into the world and thus, writing is considered thinking through fingertips.

The writer within a trainer plays a pivotal role in enhancing the training experience by creating clarity, structure, and engagement.

Here's how the "WRITER" comes to life in a trainer

W - WINS THE WORD

A writer excels at crafting compelling narratives, weaving words into stories, ideas, and emotions that deeply resonate with learners.

R - REACHABLE

By leveraging writing skills, trainers can broaden their impact through blogs, articles, or books, reaching a wider audience and solidifying their position as thought leaders.

I - IMPACTS INFLUENCE

The writer within a trainer uses storytelling to transform abstract concepts into relatable, memorable lessons. A powerful anecdote can leave a lasting impact.

T – TRANSFORMATIONAL

Strong writing amplifies a trainer's ability to move beyond the informational, turning lessons into truly transformational experiences for their audience.

E - ENGAGING

Effective trainers create clear and engaging content—whether it's lesson plans, manuals, or presentations—ensuring materials are easy to follow and captivating.

R – RESOURCEFUL

In an era of e-learning, trainers who write well can develop online courses, scripts, and interactive modules, seamlessly blending teaching with the written word.

tête-à-tête

The trainer's superpower is sharing knowledge

C*hoti: Dr. Annepaul, you said trainers have three personalities. Is it like having three secret identities, like superheroes?*

Dr. Annepaul: (smiling) That's a fun way to think about it, Choti. Trainers do wear three hats: the trainer, the coach, and the writer. Each one has its own unique purpose and power. Let me explain.

Choti: Okay! Let's start with the trainer. What's their superpower?

Dr. Annepaul: The trainer's superpower is sharing knowledge. Imagine standing in front of a group and teaching them something new, making complicated ideas simple and easy to understand. Trainers bring energy, structure, and clarity to help others learn.

Choti: So trainers are like teachers, right? What about the coach? Do they help you win games?

Dr. Annepaul: (laughs) Not quite, Choti. The coach's superpower is guiding others to discover their own answers. They don't tell you what to do—they ask questions, listen, and help you think deeply. Coaches focus on personal growth and unlocking potential.

Choti: Oh, like when my soccer coach says, "What's the best way to pass the ball?" instead of just shouting instructions?

Dr. Annepaul: Exactly! Coaching is about helping people find their own solutions. Now, the third personality—the writer—has a different superpower. Writers create stories, lessons, and ideas that inspire others. They capture thoughts and experiences in words so they can be shared with the world.

Choti: Writers sound creative! Do trainers have to write books?

Dr. Annepaul: Not always books, Choti. Trainers might write training materials, articles, or even journals. Writing helps them reflect, organize their thoughts, and share their insights with others. It's an important part of their journey.

Choti: Wow! So trainers have to teach, guide, and write. Isn't that hard to do all at once?

Dr. Annepaul: It can be challenging, but it's also rewarding. Each personality complements the others. For example, as a trainer, you share knowledge. As a coach, you deepen connections. And as a writer, you keep learning and growing. Together, they form a balanced and harmonious whole.

Choti: Do you switch between the three personalities too, Dr.

Annepaul?

Dr. Annepaul: (smiling warmly) *Every day, Choti. Sometimes I'm teaching, other times I'm coaching, and often I'm writing down what I've learned. It's part of the journey—and every trainer has their own unique path.*

Choti: Maybe I'll try being all three too, when I grow up. But for now, I'll just practice writing my thoughts like you do!

Dr. Annepaul: That's a wonderful start, Choti. Remember, each personality grows over time, just like you. Keep exploring, learning, and creating—you're already on your way.

IV

Four Walls of a Trainer (Blocks)

Writer's block can be a significant hurdle. Here are the four common types of writer's block and some strategies to overcome them, which can be useful for trainers

BLANK WALL

J ust like writers, trainers can experience their own version of "Blank Page Syndrome." Imagine standing in front of a group, ready to deliver a training session, but the words just won't come out or the ideas you prepared seem inadequate.

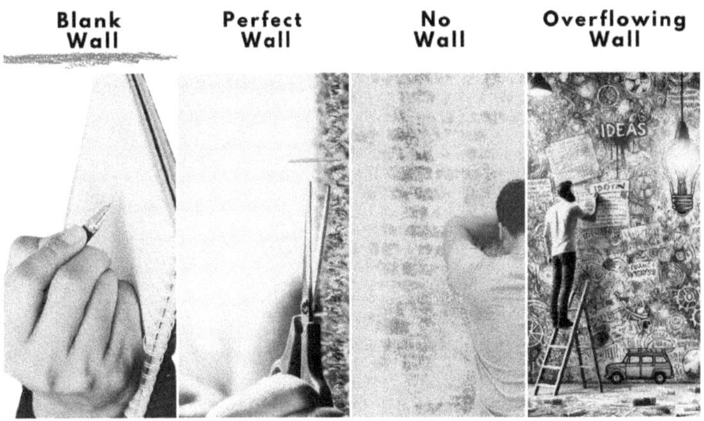

Here are some common symptoms trainers might face and some strategies to overcome them:

Symptoms of Trainer's Block

- Sudden Loss of Confidence: Feeling unsure about the material, even though you know it well.
- Creative Block: Struggling to come up with engaging activities or examples for your session.
- Overwhelm: Feeling overwhelmed by the amount of content to cover.
- Nervousness: Experiencing heightened anxiety before or during the training session.

Strategies to Overcome Trainer's Block

- Prepare your material thoroughly and rehearse your presentation multiple times.
- Use visual aids, handouts, and real-life examples to enrich your session.
- Start with an icebreaker to create a relaxed atmosphere.

- Ask open-ended questions to encourage participation and interaction.
- Divide your content into manageable sections.
- Focus on one section at a time to reduce the feeling of overwhelm.
- Take deep breaths, meditate, or practice mindfulness before your session to calm your nerves.
- Visualize a successful training session to boost your confidence.
- After your session, seek feedback from your audience or colleagues.
- Use the feedback to refine and improve future training sessions.
- Be open to adjusting your plan based on the audience's needs and responses.
- Allow yourself to deviate from the script when necessary to keep the session dynamic and engaging.

What are your top Strategies to Overcome Trainer's Block

PERFECT WALL

The Perfectionist Syndrome can be quite a hurdle for trainers, just as it is for writers. Trainers might feel an intense pressure to deliver flawless sessions, which can sometimes become paralyzing. Here's how trainers can recognize and overcome this syndrome

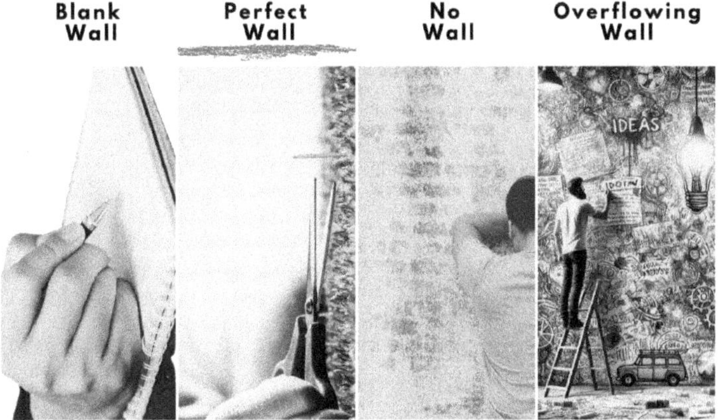

Symptoms of Perfectionist Syndrome

- Fear of Mistakes: Worrying excessively about making even minor errors during the session.
- Over Preparation: Spending an excessive amount of time preparing, often at the expense of other important tasks.
- Reluctance to Start: Delaying the start of the session or certain activities, fearing they won't be perfect.
- Constant Self Critique: Continuously doubting your abilities and replaying perceived mistakes in your mind.

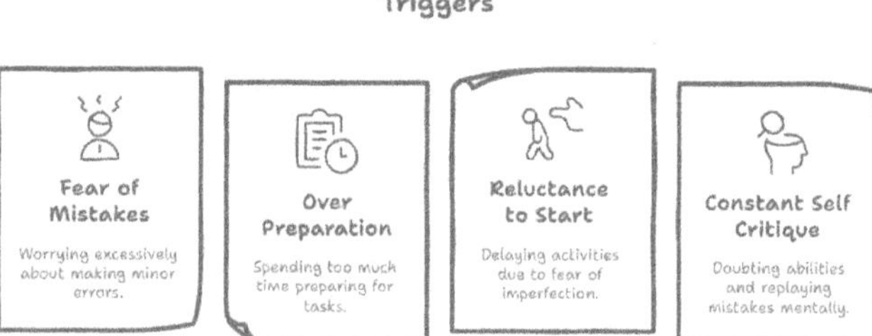

Strategies to Overcome Perfectionist Syndrome

- Aim for excellence, not perfection. Understand that no session will be flawless, and that's okay.
- Celebrate small achievements and improvements rather than fixating on what wasn't perfect.
- View mistakes as learning opportunities. Remember that they can make your sessions more relatable and authentic.

- Allocate a reasonable amount of time for preparation and stick to it. This will help you avoid over preparing.
- Treat yourself with the same kindness and understanding you would offer to others.
- Regularly seek feedback from your audience and colleagues, and use it constructively.
- Find a mentor or peer who can provide support and advice.

What are your top Strategies to Overcome Perfectionist Syndrome

NO WALL

Trainers can sometimes feel a lack of motivation or inspiration. This can be a challenging situation, but there are ways to reignite that spark.

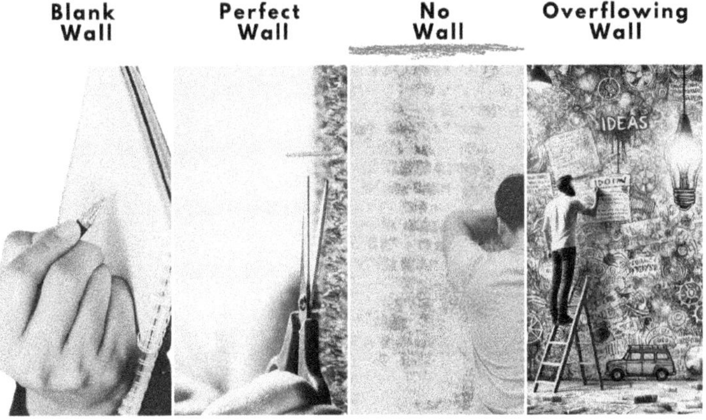

Here are some common symptoms trainers might face and some strategies to overcome them:

Symptoms of Lack of Motivation or Inspiration

- Procrastination: Delaying the preparation or delivery of training sessions.
- Monotony: Feeling that the training sessions are becoming repetitive and un engaging.
- Disinterest: Losing passion for the subject matter or the training process itself.
- Low Energy: Feeling physically and mentally drained, making it hard to bring enthusiasm to the sessions.

Factors Affecting Trainer's Engagement

Strategies to Overcome Lack of Motivation or Inspiration

- Define specific, achievable goals for each training session to give yourself a sense of purpose and direction.
- Continuously learn and update your knowledge to keep your training material fresh and interesting.
- Engage with other trainers and professionals to share ideas, experiences, and best practices.
- Use different teaching methods and tools to keep your sessions dynamic and engaging.
- Allow yourself time to rest and recharge between training sessions to avoid burnout.
- Look for inspiration from various sources such as books, articles, podcasts, or conferences related to your field.
- Remind yourself of the positive impact your training has on others and the value you bring to their learning journey.
- Involve your audience in the training process through interactive activities and discussions to make the sessions more engaging and enjoyable.

What are your top Strategies to Overcome Lack of Motivation or Inspiration

OVERFLOWING WALL

Having too many ideas can be overwhelming for trainers. It can be challenging to focus and organize your thoughts effectively.

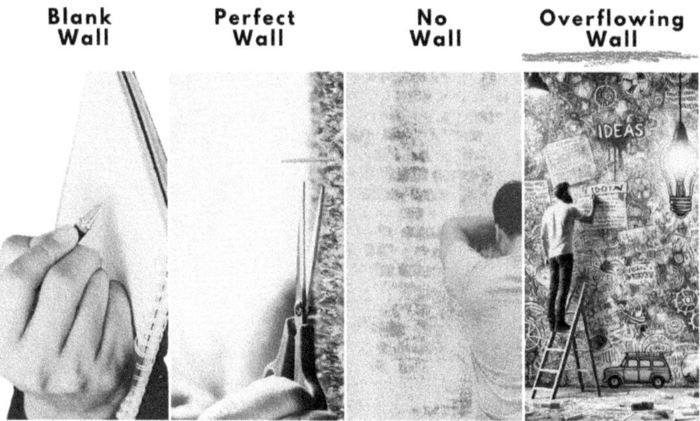

Here are some common symptoms trainers might face and some strategies to overcome them:

Symptoms of Having Too Many Ideas

- Information Overload: Feeling overwhelmed by the sheer volume of ideas and information.
- Difficulty in Prioritizing: Struggling to decide which ideas to focus on and which to set aside.
- Scattered Thoughts: Having trouble organizing ideas into a coherent and structured format.
- Procrastination: Delaying the start of a session because you're unsure where to begin.

Challenges in Idea Management

Strategies to Overcome when you are having too many Ideas

- Write down all your ideas in a list or mind map to visualize them clearly.
- Group similar ideas together and prioritize them based on relevance and importance.
- Develop a structured outline to organize your ideas into a logical flow for your session.
- Define the key objectives for your session to help you focus on the most important ideas.
- Narrow down the scope of your session to avoid covering too much information at once.
- Allocate specific time slots for each idea to ensure you stay on track and cover the essentials.
- Discuss your ideas with colleagues or peers to get their input and help refine your focus.
- Continuously review and refine your ideas and session plan based on feedback and reflection.

What are your top Strategies to Overcome when you are having too many Ideas

tête-à-tête

The best way is to focus on progress, not perfection

Choti: Dr. Annepaul, what's writer's block? Is it like a big wall that stops you from writing?

Dr. Annepaul: (smiling) That's a creative way to describe it, Choti! Writer's block happens when someone feels stuck and can't write, even when they want to. And you're right—it can feel like hitting a wall. For trainers, it can happen when writing lessons, materials, or reflections.

Choti: Trainers can get stuck too? What kind of walls do they face?

Dr. Annepaul: Trainers can face four types of walls. Let's explore them! The first one is the Blank Wall. Imagine standing in front of a blank page with no ideas coming to you—it's like staring at an empty white wall.

Choti: Oh no! What should they do if their brain feels blank?

Dr. Annepaul: They can start with small steps—jotting down anything that comes to mind, even if it feels random. Sometimes a walk, a change of scenery, or asking others for ideas can spark inspiration too.

Choti: Okay, what's the next wall?

Dr. Annepaul: The second one is the Overflowing Wall. This happens when you have too many ideas and don't know where to start. It's like trying to climb a wall with water pouring down on you.

Choti: Sounds messy! What's the fix?

Dr. Annepaul: Trainers can make lists or mind maps to organize their thoughts. Choosing the most important ideas first helps clear the chaos and create focus.

Choti: That makes sense! What about the third wall?

Dr. Annepaul: That's the No Wall. Believe it or not, this block happens when you're too distracted—your thoughts are scattered everywhere, and you can't concentrate enough to write.

Choti: Like trying to write with a noisy TV on! How do trainers deal with that?

Dr. Annepaul: They can create a quiet space and set clear goals. Even simple techniques like deep breathing or focusing on one task at a time help bring back their concentration.

Choti: Okay, and the fourth wall? Is it the hardest one?

Dr. Annepaul: The last one is the Perfect Wall. This happens when a trainer wants their writing to be perfect and gets stuck trying to make it flawless.

Choti: Oh, perfection sounds tricky! What do they do?

Dr. Annepaul: The best way is to focus on progress, not perfection. Trainers can write freely and remind themselves that revisions come later. Writing isn't about getting it perfect on the first try—it's about expressing ideas.

Choti: So trainers have four big walls to climb! But they can break through them with the right tools, right?

Dr. Annepaul: You've got it, Choti! Overcoming writer's block takes patience and practice. Every trainer has their own journey with these walls—and each time they overcome one, they grow stronger.

Choti: I think I'll try these tricks next time I get stuck in school. Thanks, Dr. Annepaul—you always know how to help!

Dr. Annepaul: (smiling warmly) You're welcome, Choti. Remember, writing is a process, and even the smallest step forward is progress. Keep climbing those walls—you're on your way to great heights!

V

Five Senses a Trainer can activate

The five senses can transform a training session into an unforgettable experience. By involving tactile activities that encourage hands-on interaction, trainers bring concepts to life. Emotional "feel," paired with storytelling, creates connections that resonate deeply. Using sound, trainers amplify focus and interest, whether through tone or auditory tools like music. Scents can sparking associations and enhancing the environment, while taste adds a playful and memorable layer to learning.

VISUAL

Visual tools enhance the learning experience by making information more engaging and easier to understand.

Here are some effective visual tools a trainer can use:

Slides and Presentations

Tools like PowerPoint or Google Slides allow trainers to create visually appealing presentations with text, images, charts, and videos. In fact, today there are many more apps like Canva which is my personal favorite.

Infographics

These are great for summarizing information and presenting data in a visually engaging way. Tools like Canva or Piktochart can help create professional-looking infographics. I am using Napkin Ai these days.

Whiteboards and Flip Charts

These traditional tools are excellent for interactive sessions, brainstorming, and illustrating concepts in real-time. In all my trainings, i make sure to have a flip board and colorful markers—a fun and simple way to put down my thoughts

Videos

Incorporating videos can help explain complex topics, provide real-world examples, and keep learners engaged. Platforms like YouTube or Vimeo offer a vast library of educational videos.

Diagrams and Charts

Visual representations of data, processes, or structures can make complex information more digestible. Tools like Lucidchart or Microsoft Visio are useful for creating diagrams and flowcharts.

Mind Maps

These help in organizing information visually, showing relationships between different concepts. Tools like MindMeister or XMind can be used to create digital mind maps.

Interactive Tools

Tools like Kahoot! or Mentimeter allow trainers to create interactive quizzes and polls, making sessions more engaging and participatory.

Virtual Reality (VR) and Augmented Reality (AR)

These advanced tools can provide immersive learning experiences, especially useful for simulations and hands-on training.

Handouts and Worksheets

Visual handouts and worksheets can reinforce learning and provide a reference for learners to review later.

Graphic Organizers

Tools like Venn diagrams, flow charts, and concept maps help learners organize and visualize information.

Diagrams and Charts

Videos

Mind Maps

ICEBREAKERS

Here are some engaging icebreakers that can activate the sense of visuals and get participants excited:

1. Picture Prompt

Provide participants with a random image and ask them to create a story or describe what they see. This encourages creativity and visual thinking.

2. Visual Pictionary

Divide participants into teams and have them draw clues for their teammates to guess. Use a whiteboard or digital drawing tool like Jamboard for this activity.

3. Emoji Story

Ask participants to create a short story using only emojis. This can be done on paper or digitally, and it's a fun way to engage visual and creative skills.

4. Color Code

Give each participant a colored card and ask them to find others with the same color. Once grouped, they can discuss a topic or answer a question related to the training session.

5. Visual Quiz

Use tools like Kahoot! or Mentimeter to create a quiz with images. Participants can answer questions based on the visuals, making the activity interactive and engaging.

6. Mind Map Creation

Provide a central topic and ask participants to create a mind map using visuals and keywords. Tools like MindMeister or XMind can be used for digital mind maps.

7. Infographic Challenge

Give participants a topic and ask them to create an infographic summarizing key points. Tools like Canva or Piktochart can be used for this activity.

8. Photo Scavenger Hunt

Create a list of items or themes and ask participants to take photos that represent each one. This can be done individually or in teams, and it's a great way to get everyone moving and thinking visually.

9. Visual Storytelling

Show a series of images and ask participants to create a narrative connecting them. This can be done in groups or individually, and it encourages imaginative thinking.

10. Sketch and Share

Ask participants to sketch their thoughts or ideas on a given topic and then share their drawings with the group. This can be done on paper or using digital drawing tools.

Create your own ONE icebreaker to activate the sense of SIGHT

HEAR

Auditory tools can greatly enhance the learning experience by engaging learners through sound. Here are some effective auditory tools a trainer can use:

Podcasts

Creating or recommending relevant podcasts can provide learners with valuable insights and information in an engaging audio format.

Audio Recordings

Recording lectures, instructions, or explanations allows learners to listen and review the material at their own pace. Tools like Audacity or even smartphone voice recorders can be used for this purpose.

Music and Sound Effects

Using background music or sound effects can set the tone for a session, enhance engagement, and create a more immersive learning environment.

Voice Modulation

Trainers can use their own voice effectively by varying pitch, tone, and pace to emphasize key points and maintain learner interest.

Interactive Voice Response (IVR)

This technology can be used for automated training modules where learners interact with a system through voice commands.

Audiobooks

Recommending or providing audiobooks related to the training topic can offer an alternative way for learners to absorb information.

Webinars and Live Sessions

Hosting live audio sessions or webinars allows for real-time interaction and engagement with learners. Platforms like Zoom or Microsoft Teams are great for this.

Language Learning Apps

For language training, apps like Duolingo or Rosetta Stone use auditory tools to help learners practice listening and speaking skills.

Speech-to-Text Tools

Tools like Dragon NaturallySpeaking can help trainers create written content from spoken words, which can then be shared with learners.

Interactive Voice Quizzes

Tools like Kahoot! or Quizlet can be used to create voice-based quizzes, making the learning process more interactive and fun.

Podcast
Music and Sound Effects
Audio Recordings
Voice Modulation
Interactive Voice Response (IVR)
Audiobooks
Webinars and Live Sessions
Speech-to-Text Tools
Language Learning Apps
Interactive Voice Quizzes

ICEBREAKERS

Here are some engaging icebreakers that can activate the sense of auditory and get participants excited:

1. Sound Scavenger Hunt

Play various sounds (e.g., animal noises, musical instruments, nature sounds) and ask participants to identify them. This can be done using audio clips from the internet or a soundboard app.

2. Two Truths and a Lie (Audio Edition)

Participants share two true statements and one false statement about themselves, but they record these statements as audio clips. The group listens to the clips and guesses which statement is the lie.

3. Audio Story Chain

Start a story and record the first sentence. Pass the recording to the next participant, who adds another sentence, and so on. Play the final story for the group to enjoy.

4. Guess the Song

Play short clips of popular songs and have participants guess the title and artist. This can be a fun and energetic way to start a session.

5. Voice Modulation Exercise

Have participants introduce themselves using different voice modulations (e.g., high pitch, low pitch, fast, slow). This can be both fun and a great way to practice vocal variety.

6. Soundtrack of Your Life

Ask participants to choose a song that represents their life or current mood and explain why. Play a short clip of each song as they share their stories.

7. Audio Charades

Participants act out a word or phrase using only sounds and noises (no words). The rest of the group guesses what they are trying to convey.

8. Podcast Pitch

In small groups, participants come up with an idea for a podcast and record a short pitch. Play the pitches for the group and vote on the most interesting one.

9. Mystery Sound Box

Fill a box with various objects that make distinct sounds. Participants take turns shaking the box and guessing what's inside based on the sound.

10. Echo Game

One participant says a word or phrase, and the next person repeats it with a slight variation in tone or pitch. Continue around the group, creating an auditory chain.

Create your own ONE icebreaker to activate the sense of HEARING

HEAR

TOUCH

I ncorporating the sense of touch into training sessions can enhance the learning experience by making it more interactive and engaging. Here are some tactile tools and techniques a trainer can use:

Hands-On Activities

Engaging learners in activities that require physical manipulation, such as assembling models, using tools, or crafting, can reinforce learning through touch.

Interactive Demonstrations

Allowing learners to participate in demonstrations where they can touch and handle materials or equipment helps them understand concepts better.

Physical Props

Using tangible objects related to the training topic can make abstract concepts more concrete. For example, using anatomical models in medical training.

Simulations

Creating realistic simulations where learners can practice skills in a controlled environment can be highly effective. This is common in fields like healthcare, aviation, and emergency response.

Tactile Learning Aids

Providing materials like textured flashcards, braille resources, or 3D-printed models can support learners who benefit from tactile input.

Role-Playing

Encouraging learners to act out scenarios or practice skills in role-playing exercises can make the learning experience more immersive and hands-on.

Workshops

Conducting workshops where learners can engage in practical, hands-on tasks related to the training topic can enhance their understanding and retention.

Interactive Whiteboards

Using interactive whiteboards that learners can touch and manipulate can make sessions more dynamic and engaging.

Physical Movement

Incorporating activities that involve physical movement, such as group exercises, games, or kinaesthetic learning activities, can help learners stay engaged and retain information better.

Sensory Kits

Providing kits that include various tactile materials, such as fabrics, tools, or samples, can enhance sensory learning and exploration.

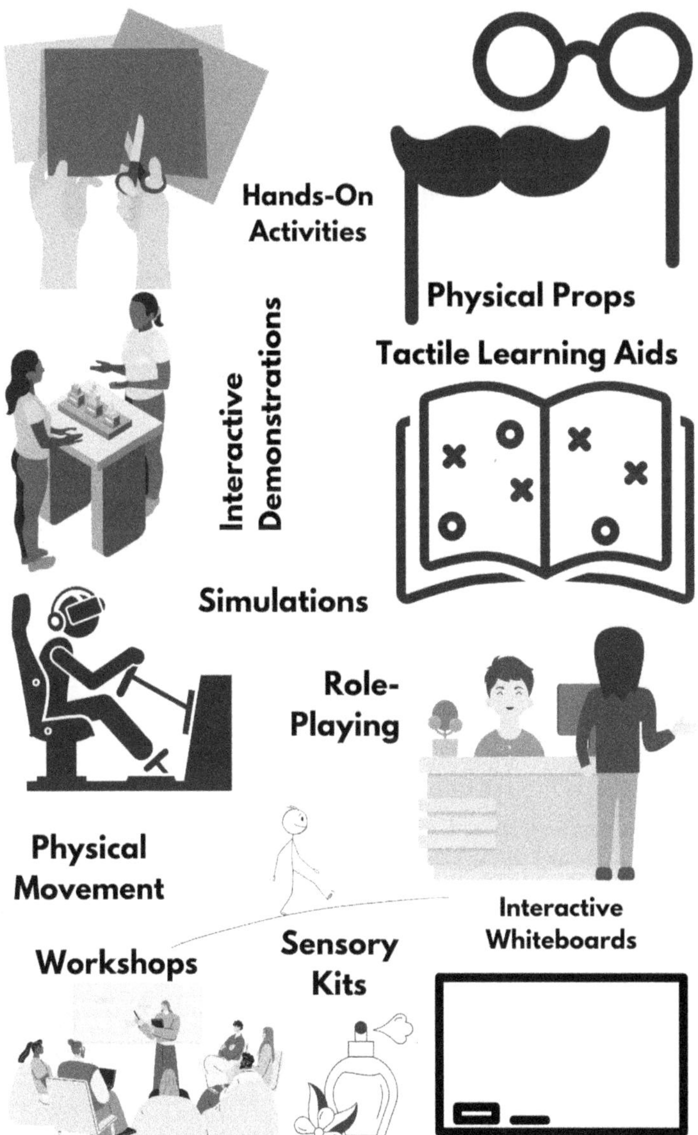
Hands-On
Activities
Physical Props
Tactile Learning Aids
Interactive
Demonstrations
Simulations
Role-
Playing
Physical
Movement
Interactive
Whiteboards
Workshops
Sensory
Kits

ICEBREAKERS

Here are some engaging icebreakers that can activate the sense of touch and get participants excited:

1. Mystery Box

Fill a box with various objects and have participants reach in and guess what they are touching without looking. This can be a fun way to start a session and stimulate tactile senses.

2. Clay Creations

Provide participants with modelling clay and ask them to create something related to the training topic. This hands-on activity encourages creativity and tactile engagement.

3. Touch and Tell

Pass around different textured objects (e.g., sandpaper, silk, sponge) and have participants describe how each one feels. This can lead to interesting discussions about sensory experiences.

4. Building Challenge

Give participants materials like LEGO bricks, blocks, or other building tools and challenge them to construct something within a time limit. This promotes teamwork and tactile interaction.

5. Sensory Relay

Set up a relay race where participants have to complete tasks involving touch, such as feeling for specific objects in a bag or assembling a puzzle blindfolded.

6. Tactile Storytelling

Provide various tactile materials (e.g., fabric swatches, textured paper) and ask participants to create a story or scene using these materials. This can be done individually or in groups.

7. Puzzle Pieces

Give each participant a piece of a puzzle and ask them to find others with matching pieces to complete the puzzle together. This encourages collaboration and tactile engagement.

8. Craft Corner

Set up a craft station with materials like paper, scissors, glue, and markers, and ask participants to create something related to the training topic. This hands-on activity can be both relaxing and engaging.

9. Interactive Map

Create a large map related to the training topic and provide tactile markers (e.g., stickers, pins) for participants to place on the map as they discuss different areas or concepts.

10. Sensory Walk

Set up a path with different textures (e.g., carpet, grass, pebbles) and have participants walk barefoot along it, discussing how each texture feels underfoot. This can be a refreshing way to engage the sense of touch.

Create your own ONE icebreaker to activate the sense of TOUCH

TASTE

Incorporating taste into training sessions can create a memorable and engaging learning experience. Here are some tools and ideas trainers can use to activate the sense of taste:

Food and Beverages

Providing snacks or drinks related to the training topic can make sessions more enjoyable. For example, offering different types of tea during a session on cultural diversity.

Taste Tests

Conducting taste tests can be a fun and interactive way to engage learners. This is particularly useful in training related to food, nutrition, or sensory evaluation.

Cooking Demonstrations

For training sessions related to culinary arts or nutrition, live cooking demonstrations can be an effective way to engage learners through taste.

Edible Rewards

Using small edible rewards, like candies or chocolates, can motivate learners and make the training experience more enjoyable.

Themed Meals

Organizing themed meals or snacks that align with the training topic can enhance the learning experience. For example, serving Italian cuisine during a session on Italian culture.

Interactive Food Activities

Incorporating activities where learners prepare or taste food can be highly engaging. This is especially useful in hands-on training sessions.

Sensory Kits

Providing sensory kits that include various food items for tasting can help learners explore different flavours and textures. This is useful in sensory training or food science education.

Pairing Exercises

Conducting exercises where learners pair different foods and beverages can enhance their understanding of taste combinations and sensory experiences.

Culinary Field Trips

Organizing visits to local food markets, restaurants, or culinary schools can provide learners with real-world taste experiences related to the training topic.

Taste Descriptions

Encouraging learners to describe and discuss their taste experiences can enhance their sensory awareness and communication skills.

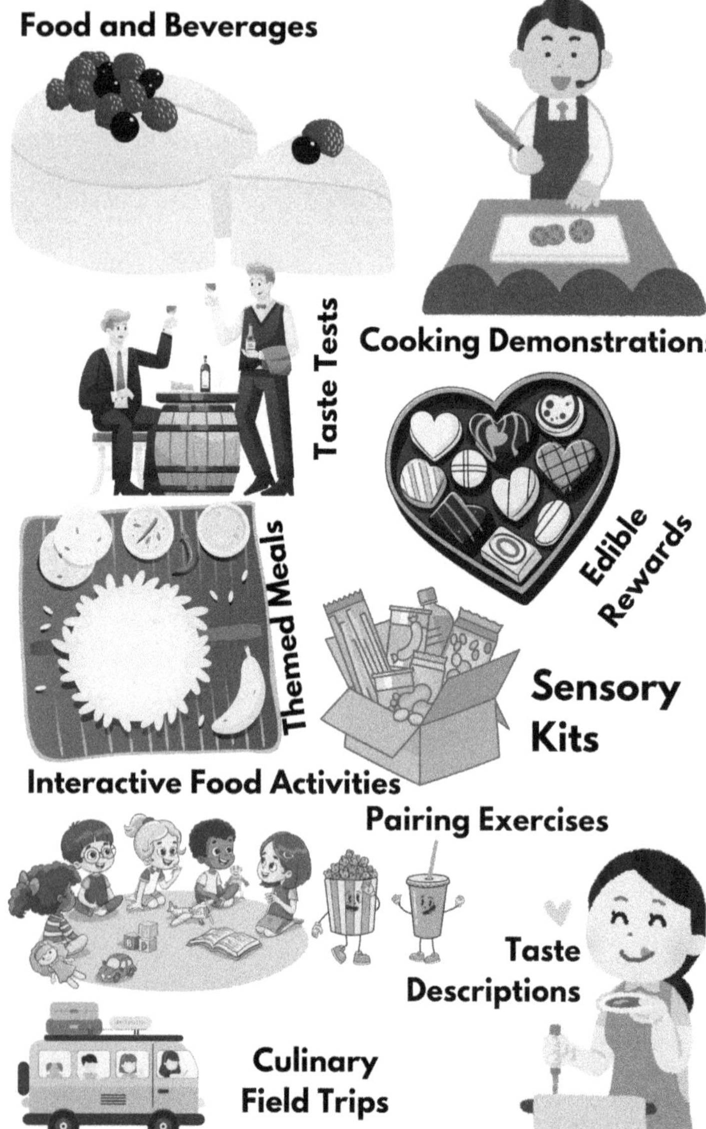
Food and Beverages
Cooking Demonstrations
Taste Tests
Edible Rewards
Themed Meals
Sensory Kits
Interactive Food Activities
Pairing Exercises
Taste Descriptions
Culinary Field Trips

ICEBREAKERS

Here are some engaging icebreakers that can activate the sense of taste and make your training sessions more memorable:

1. Blind Taste Test

Provide a variety of foods or beverages and have participants taste them blindfolded. They can guess the flavors and discuss their experiences. This is a fun way to engage the sense of taste and encourage discussion.

2. Flavor Pairing Challenge

Give participants different foods and ask them to create unique flavor combinations. They can then share their creations and explain why they think the flavors work well together.

3. Cultural Taste Exploration

Offer samples of foods from different cultures and have participants guess the country of origin. This can lead to interesting discussions about cultural diversity and culinary traditions.

4. Taste and Tell

Ask participants to bring a small sample of their favorite snack or dish. They can share it with the group and explain why they like it. This is a great way to learn more about each other and share personal stories.

5. Edible Name Tags

Provide edible items like cookies or fruit slices and edible markers. Have participants write their names on the items and then share them with the group. This is a fun and interactive way to introduce everyone.

6. Mystery Ingredient

Prepare a dish with a secret ingredient and have participants taste it and guess what the mystery ingredient is. This can be a fun and engaging way to start a session.

7. Flavor Memory Game

Provide a selection of foods with distinct flavors. Have participants taste each one and then try to remember and match the flavors after a short break. This can be a fun way to test memory and sensory perception.

8. Recipe Swap

Ask participants to bring a favorite recipe and a small sample of the dish. They can swap recipes and taste each other's creations. This is a great way to share culinary skills and discover new dishes.

9. Taste Bingo

Create bingo cards with different flavors or food items. As participants taste each item, they can mark it off on their cards. The first to complete a row or column wins a small prize.

10. Flavor Wheel

Provide a flavor wheel with different taste categories (e.g., sweet, salty, sour, bitter). Have participants taste various foods and place them on the wheel. This can help them understand and appreciate different flavor profiles.

Create your own ONE icebreaker to activate the sense of TASTE

TASTE

SMELL

I ncorporating the sense of smell into training sessions can create a unique and memorable learning experience. Here are some tools and techniques a trainer can use to activate the sense of smell:

Aromatherapy

Using essential oils or scented candles can create a calming or stimulating environment, depending on the training context. Scents like lavender can promote relaxation, while citrus scents can enhance alertness.

Scented Markers and Pens

Providing scented markers or pens can make activities like drawing or writing more engaging and enjoyable for learners.

Scented Samples

For training related to food, beverages, or perfumes, providing scented samples can help learners better understand and appreciate different aromas.

Scented Objects

Incorporating objects with distinct smells, such as herbs, spices, or flowers, can enhance sensory learning and make abstract concepts more tangible.

Smell Kits

Creating kits with various scented items can be useful for activities that involve identifying or describing different smells. This is particularly useful in training related to sensory evaluation or culinary arts.

Environmental Scents

Using diffusers or air fresheners to introduce specific scents into the training environment can set the mood and enhance the overall experience. For example, using a pine scent during a session on nature or outdoor activities.

Interactive Smell Activities

Designing activities where learners have to identify or match scents can be both fun and educational. This can be particularly effective in training related to food, beverages, or fragrances.

Scented Stickers

Using scented stickers as rewards or part of interactive activities can add an element of fun and engagement to the training session.

Scented Learning Materials

Incorporating scents into learning materials, such as scratch-and-sniff cards or scented paper, can make the learning experience more immersive.

Field Trips

Organizing visits to places with distinct smells, such as botanical gardens, food markets, or factories, can provide learners with real-world sensory experiences related to the training topic.

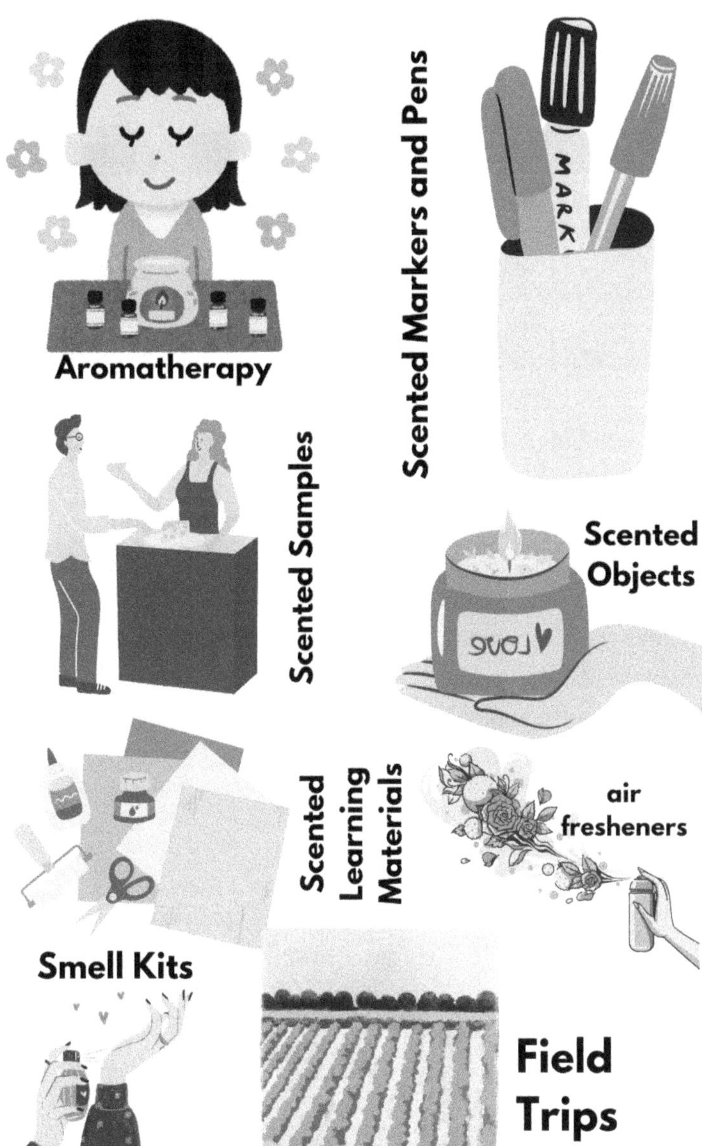
Aromatherapy
Scented Markers and Pens
Scented Samples
Scented Objects
LOVE
Scented Learning Materials
air fresheners
Smell Kits
Field Trips

ICEBREAKERS

Here are some engaging icebreakers that can activate the sense of smell and make your training sessions more memorable:

1. Mystery Scent Jars

Fill small jars with various scents (e.g., coffee, vanilla, cinnamon, lavender) and have participants smell each jar and guess the scent. This can be a fun way to start a session and stimulate the sense of smell.

2. Scented Storytelling

Provide participants with different scented items (e.g., herbs, spices, essential oils) and ask them to create a short story inspired by the scent. This encourages creativity and sensory engagement.

3. Aromatherapy Introduction

Introduce different essential oils and explain their benefits. Allow participants to smell each oil and discuss how the scents make them feel. This can be a relaxing and informative activity.

4. Scent Matching Game

Prepare pairs of scented items and mix them up. Have participants find the matching scents by smelling each item. This can be a fun and interactive way to engage the sense of smell.

5. Scented Memory Game

Create cards with different scents and have participants match the cards based on the smell. This can be a fun way to test memory and sensory perception.

6. Herb and Spice Exploration

Provide a variety of herbs and spices for participants to smell and identify. This can be particularly engaging for training sessions related to cooking or nutrition.

7. Scented Icebreaker Questions

Use scented markers or pens to write icebreaker questions on cards. Participants can choose a card, smell the scent, and answer the question. This adds an extra sensory element to the activity.

8. Scented Relaxation Exercise

Guide participants through a relaxation exercise using calming scents like lavender or chamomile. This can help set a positive and relaxed tone for the session.

9. Perfume Sampling

Provide samples of different perfumes or colognes and have participants describe the scents and choose their favorites. This can be a fun and engaging way to explore different aromas.

10. Scented Art

Give participants scented markers or paints and ask them to create artwork inspired by the scents. This combines visual and olfactory senses for a unique creative experience.

Create your own ONE icebreaker to activate the sense of SMELL

tête-à-tête

Engaging all five senses—touch, feel, hear, smell, and taste—can turn an ordinary session into an unforgettable experience

C *hoti: Dr. Annepaul, do trainers really use all five senses? I thought training was just about talking and listening.*

Dr. Annepaul: Oh, Choti, trainers can do so much more! Engaging all five senses—touch, feel, hear, smell, and taste—can turn an ordinary session into an unforgettable experience. Let me show you how.

Choti: Okay, let's start with touch! How does touch help in training?

Dr. Annepaul: Touch is about hands-on interaction. For example, a trainer might use props, tools, or materials that participants can handle. It could be as simple as writing on a board or assembling something during an activity. Touch helps learners connect physically with what they're learning.

Choti: That sounds fun! What about "feel"? Isn't that more about emotions?

Dr. Annepaul: Exactly, Choti. "Feel" is about emotional connection. Trainers can share meaningful stories or examples that evoke emotions like curiosity, excitement, or empathy. When participants feel something deeply, they're more likely to remember and understand the lesson.

Choti: So if they feel happy or curious, they'll learn better? I like that!

Dr. Annepaul: That's right. Now, let's talk about hearing. Trainers use their voice to teach, but they can also include music, sound effects, or even quiet moments to keep participants' attention. The tone, pitch, and rhythm of their voice can make a big difference too.

Choti: I'd love to hear a story with sound effects—like thunder or birds chirping! What about smell? Can you really use smell in training?

Dr. Annepaul: Smell can set the mood. Imagine the scent of lavender creating a calming atmosphere during a reflective session, or citrus to energize the group. Smells can also trigger memories, making the session more memorable.

Choti: Wow! And how does taste fit into training? Trainers don't feed everyone cake, do they?

Dr. Annepaul: (laughs) Not always, Choti! But taste can be used creatively. For example, a trainer could bring snacks related to the theme of the session—like regional foods for cultural training—or use taste to create metaphors. Even a small treat can make learning more enjoyable.

Choti: That sounds delicious! So trainers use all these senses to make learning fun and interesting?

Dr. Annepaul: Exactly, Choti. Engaging the senses helps participants stay focused, involved, and inspired. It's not just about facts and figures—it's about creating an experience that stays with them.

Choti: I think that's amazing, Dr. Annepaul. When I grow up, I'll make sure all my training sessions smell like chocolate and sound like music!

Dr. Annepaul: (smiling warmly) I'm sure your sessions will be a delight, Choti. Keep dreaming big—you already have a creative touch.

VI

Six NLP BRANDS

Let's think of NLP as a fun way to understand and change how we think, talk, and act.
***Neuro** : Imagine your brain is like a big computer that helps you see, hear, feel, taste, and smell the world around you. This is how you experience everything!* **Linguistic:** *This is all about the words you use when you talk to others and yourself. It's like the language of your thoughts and feelings.*
***Programming** : Think of this as the way your brain learns to do things based on your experiences. It's like create*

BELIEF CHANGE

B elief change is the process of altering what we hold to be true, whether it's about ourselves, others, or the world. Shifting beliefs can happen gradually through experiences, education, or exposure to new perspectives—or suddenly, through pivotal moments or realizations.

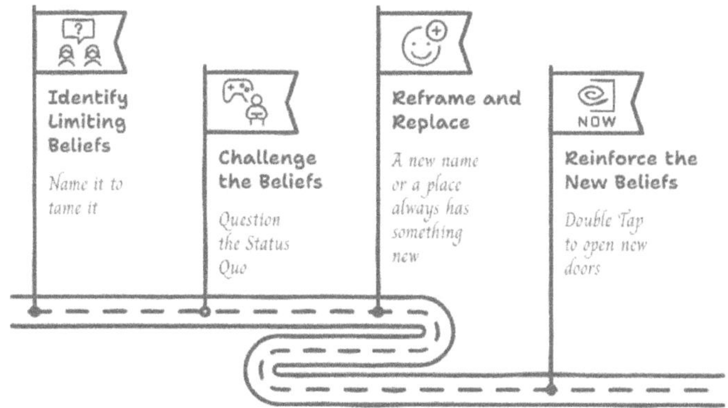

A trainer can harness the concept of belief change to profoundly impact the learning process and inspire participants to embrace new perspectives or approaches.

Here are some key strategies:

Challenge Limiting Beliefs

Trainers can help participants recognize beliefs that may be holding them back, such as "I can't learn this skill" or "This won't work for me." By creating a safe and supportive environment, they can encourage participants to question these assumptions and explore alternative viewpoints.

Incorporate Stories and Examples

Sharing stories of people who successfully overcame challenges or changed their beliefs can motivate participants. Real-world examples serve as powerful evidence of the potential for growth and transformation.

Facilitate Cognitive Reframing

Trainers can use activities or discussions to help participants reframe negative or unproductive beliefs into constructive ones. For instance, turning "Failure means I'm not good enough" into "Failure is an opportunity to learn and improve."

Introduce Experiential Learning

Belief change often happens through experience. Hands-on activities, simulations, or role-playing exercises allow participants to "live" new perspectives, making belief shifts more tangible and impactful.

Encourage Reflection

Providing space for participants to reflect on their current beliefs, explore their origins, and evaluate their validity can be transformative. Reflection fosters self-awareness, a key step toward belief change.

Create a Growth-Oriented Mindset

Trainers can emphasize the importance of adaptability and continuous learning. Highlighting the idea that beliefs are not fixed, but can evolve, encourages participants to remain open-minded.

Use Affirmations and Positive Reinforcement

Reaffirming participants' strengths and encouraging positive self-talk can reinforce new, empowering beliefs.

When trainers integrate these techniques, they not only help participants acquire new skills but also foster personal growth and resilience.

Think of a limiting belief or thought or statement or word

Replace with a positive belief or thought or statement or word

Visualise the positive belief or thought or statement or word

Write 5 Steps to reach that visualised positive belief or thought or statement or word

REFRAMING

Reframing is a powerful psychological tool that involves changing the way we perceive a situation, belief, or thought. It doesn't change the actual facts, but it alters the meaning we ascribe to them, often leading to a more constructive or empowering perspective.

Reframing is a highly effective tool trainers can use to help participants see challenges or concepts from a new, empowering perspective. Here's how a trainer can incorporate reframing into their sessions:

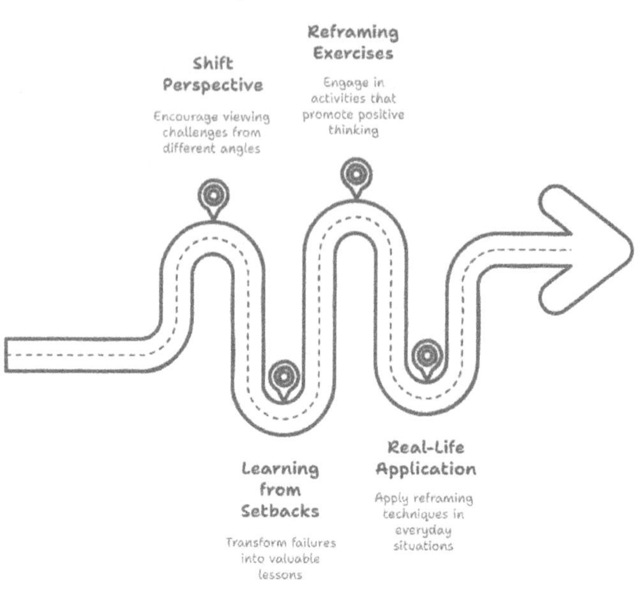

Reframe Negative Beliefs

When participants express limiting beliefs like "I can't do this," the trainer can respond with a reframe like, "You haven't mastered it yet, but that's why we're here—to grow and improve together." Encourage participants to view mistakes as learning opportunities instead of failures.

Use Thought-Provoking Questions

Ask open-ended questions that guide participants to view a situation differently. For example, "What's another way to look at this challenge?" or "How could this experience actually benefit you?"

Provide New Contexts

Share real-world examples or analogies to reframe thinking. For instance, if participants see change as a threat, present it as an opportunity for innovation and growth by likening it to evolution in nature.

Turn Problems into Possibilities

Reframe challenges as stepping stones. For example, instead of "We lack resources," a trainer could guide participants to think, "How can we creatively maximize what we do have?"

Model Reframing

Demonstrate reframing in your own language and approach. If a technical issue arises during the session, you could say, "This is a great chance to practice adaptability," rather than viewing it as a setback.

Role-Playing Activities

Incorporate exercises where participants practice reframing scenarios. For example, have them work in pairs to turn negative statements into positive or growth-oriented ones.

Encourage Journaling or Reflection

Ask participants to reflect on past situations where a belief shift or reframe changed their outcomes. This reinforces the value of reframing in their own experiences.

Celebrate Reframed Mindsets

Acknowledge and praise participants when they successfully adopt a new perspective. Positive reinforcement cements the practice of reframing.

By integrating reframing techniques, trainers empower participants to develop resilience, adaptability, and a positive outlook—skills that extend beyond the training room into their personal and professional lives.

Identify a negative thought you wish to reframe

Challenge the thought by asking, is this entirely true or just my perspective

Replace the negative thought with the most empowering alternative

Write 5 Steps to reach that replaced alternative

ANCHORING

nchoring is a powerful **NLP (Neuro-Linguistic Programming) technique** that helps individuals access desired emotional states quickly by associating them with a specific trigger (stimulus).

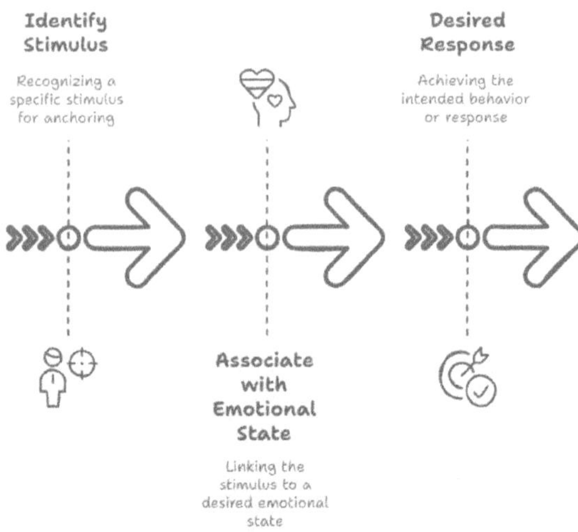

Anchoring, in the context of training and psychology, refers to the process of associating a specific stimulus with a desired emotional state, behavior, or response. It's like creating a mental "trigger" that participants can use to access a certain mindset or feeling.

How Trainers Can Use Anchoring:

Creating Positive Associations:

Use music, phrases, or visuals to evoke specific emotions. For example, a motivational song played during an inspiring moment can later serve as an anchor for participants to recall that energy and confidence.

Using Physical Anchors:

Encourage participants to associate a physical action, like clenching a fist, with a positive emotion or state, such as determination. They can then use that action later to "trigger" that feeling in challenging situations.

Connecting Emotions to Learning:

Tie key concepts to strong emotions or memorable experiences. For example, sharing a powerful story or running a high-energy activity can anchor those emotions to the training content.

Reinforcing Desired States:

If participants feel particularly confident or accomplished after an activity, ask them to identify the moment and associate it with a sensory anchor (e.g., touching their wrist or repeating a word). This helps reinforce that state for future use.

Leveraging Environmental Anchors:

Trainers can use consistent cues, like a specific seating arrangement, an object on the table, or even scents, to create an association with focus or creativity.

Anchoring for Group Dynamics:

Introduce team rituals or shared phrases that anchor a sense of unity and collaboration. These can strengthen group cohesion both during and after the training.

Practicing Anchor Activation:

Guide participants to actively use their anchors in different scenarios. For instance, if they've anchored confidence to a phrase like "I've got this," encourage them to practice saying it before presentations or challenges.

Anchoring, when used effectively, can help participants sustain motivation, access resources like confidence or focus, and integrate what they've learned into their everyday lives.

Choose a specific emotional state or response you want to anchor

Recall a powerful memory or experience where you felt that desired state vividly

Intensify the feeling by fully immersing yourself in the memory—focus on sights, sounds, and emotions

Apply a unique physical stimulus (e.g., pressing a finger to your palm or a specific gesture) at the peak of the emotion

Repeat the process with consistent practice to strengthen the anchor and make it reliable for future use

NEURO-ASSOCIATIVE CONDITIONING

Neuro-Associative Conditioning (NAC) is a psychological approach popularized by Tony Robbins, designed to help individuals create lasting behavioral change by linking pain and pleasure to specific actions, thoughts, or habits. It builds upon the principles of Neuro-Linguistic Programming (NLP) and classical conditioning. The core idea is that by changing the emotional associations tied to a behavior or belief, you can rewire your responses to align with your desired outcomes.

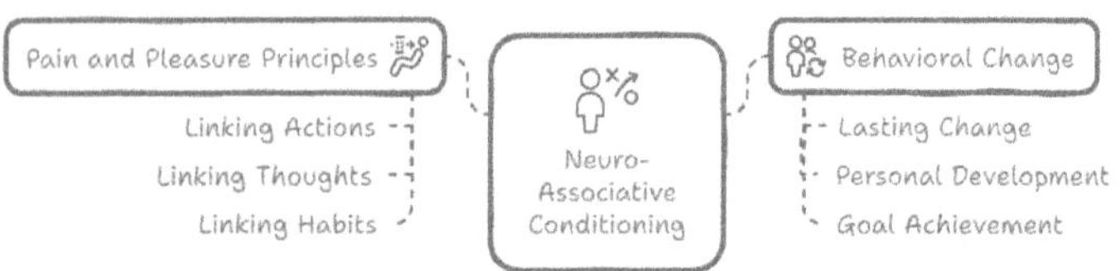

A trainer can effectively integrate Neuro-Associative Conditioning (NAC) into training sessions to drive lasting behavioral change and instill positive habits. Here's how they can apply NAC principles:

Identify Current Associations

Start by helping participants uncover their current pain and pleasure associations with certain behaviors or beliefs. For example, ask reflective questions like, "What do you associate with failure or success?" or "What holds you back from embracing change?"

Create New Empowering Associations

Guide participants to rewire their emotions by linking positive feelings to desired behaviors. For instance, trainers can use visualization exercises where participants imagine vividly achieving their goals and the joy that comes with it.

Interrupt Negative Patterns

Incorporate activities to disrupt limiting beliefs or unhelpful habits. For example, when someone defaults to "I can't do this," a trainer could employ humor, surprise, or a thought-provoking question to interrupt that automatic response.

Use Emotional Intensity

Create high-energy moments during training to make new behaviors or beliefs more emotionally impactful. This could involve passionate storytelling, role-playing exercises, or group challenges that evoke strong positive emotions.

Anchor Positive States

Teach participants to associate a specific action, word, or sensation with a positive state. For example, clenching a fist while saying "I am capable!" can act as a trigger for confidence in challenging situations.

Leverage Contrasts

Use contrasting experiences to highlight the pain of staying the same versus the pleasure of change. For instance, ask participants to imagine how life will look if they don't change a behavior, and then how life could transform if they embrace the desired change.

Reinforce Change

Help participants practice and revisit their new associations repeatedly to strengthen the neural pathways. The more they rehearse, the more automatic these behaviors and thoughts become.

Encourage Application Beyond Training

Empower participants to implement NAC in their personal and professional lives. Provide techniques they can use to self-coach, such as visualizing success, creating anchors, and interrupting negative self-talk.

By employing NAC strategies, trainers can create transformative experiences that not only teach skills but also

inspire deep emotional and mental shifts in participants.

Pinpoint a specific emotion, behavior or belief you wish to transform.

Break the current pattern by introducing a disruptive stimulus, like a physical action

Replace the old pattern with a new pattern consistently with positive affirmations to acquire the desired behavior

Visualize the future you desire, focusing on how you'll feel, act, and think once the change is fully realized

List action tools – repetitive practice, emotional triggers, or physical gestures to solidify the new behavior

DISSOCIATION

Dissociation, in psychological terms, refers to a mental process where a person disconnects from their thoughts, feelings, memories, or sense of identity. It's often a coping mechanism in response to stress, trauma, or overwhelming situations, allowing individuals to distance themselves from intense emotions or experiences.

A trainer can strategically use dissociation to help participants gain clarity, reduce emotional bias, and adopt alternative perspectives during training. Here are some practical ways dissociation can be applied

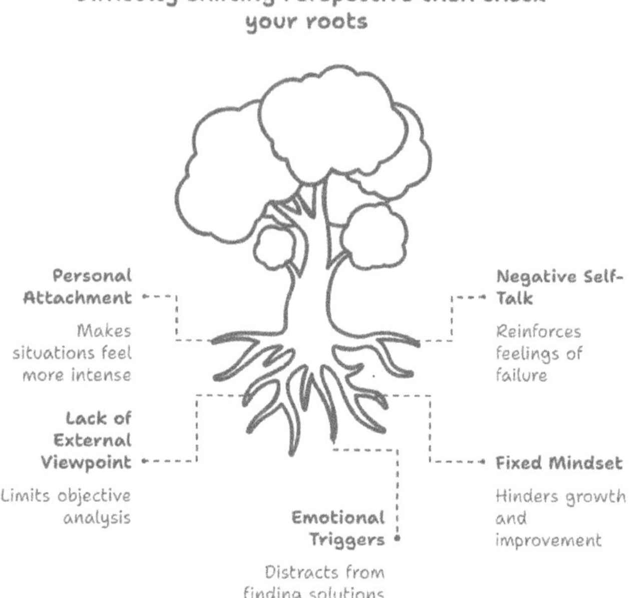

Promote Objective Problem-Solving

Encourage participants to mentally step back from a challenge and view it as an external observer. This approach helps reduce emotional entanglement and fosters rational, solution-focused thinking.

Facilitate Conflict Resolution

During exercises on conflict resolution or communication, ask participants to step into the role of an outsider observing the interaction. This can help them identify the needs and motivations of each party more objectively.

Use Visualization Exercises

Guide participants through visualization techniques where they imagine watching themselves in a situation, such as giving a presentation or handling a tough conversation. By viewing the scene from a third-person perspective, they can better analyze their behavior and performance.

Encourage Perspective-Taking

Assign participants roles or personas during simulations. For example, in a customer service training, ask them to dissociate by assuming the customer's perspective to understand their emotions and expectations.

Reframe Emotional Reactions

Teach participants to dissociate from strong emotional responses by imagining themselves as spectators of their own experiences. This can be particularly helpful in stress management or emotional intelligence training.

Analyze Group Dynamics

After group activities, encourage participants to reflect on the experience as though they were outside observers. This helps them identify effective and ineffective behaviors within the group without personal bias.

Develop Self-Awareness

Ask participants to dissociate during self-assessment exercises. For example, they can imagine how a mentor or neutral third party might perceive their strengths and areas for improvement.

Apply Storytelling

Share stories or case studies and ask participants to analyze them from an outside perspective. This creates a safe, dissociated way to explore sensitive issues and learn from them.

Dissociation, when used thoughtfully, enables participants to detach from limiting emotions or fixed perspectives, empowering them to approach situations with greater clarity and creativity.

Identify an emotion or situation causing distress

Imagine yourself as an observer, viewing the situation from a distance

Separate your feelings from the event, focusing instead on facts or logic

Create a mental image of placing the emotion away, like in a box or container

Redirect your attention to a neutral or calming activity to reinforce the dissociation

SWISH PATTERN

The Swish Pattern is a powerful Neuro-Linguistic Programming (NLP) technique designed to replace negative thought patterns with empowering ones. It works by quickly shifting mental images, helping individuals break unwanted behaviors or emotional responses and replace them with a positive mindset.

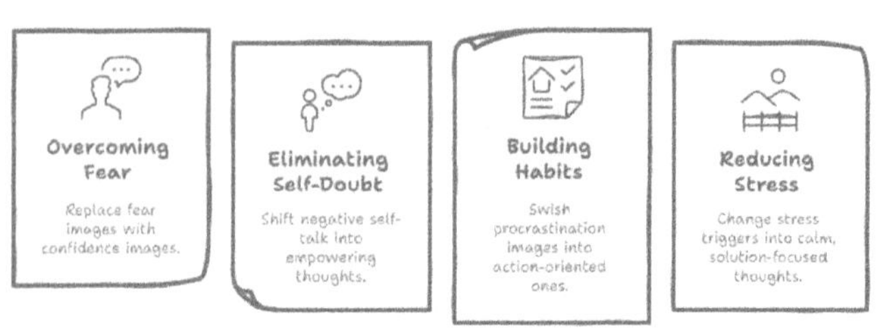

The Swish Pattern is a powerful technique from Neuro-Linguistic Programming (NLP) used to replace unwanted behaviors or thoughts with positive alternatives. It works by "reprogramming" the mind to associate the old habit or thought with a new, empowering mental image. Trainers can incorporate this technique to help participants overcome limiting habits, fears, or negative self-talk. Here's how a trainer can use the Swish Pattern effectively:

Identify the Trigger and the Desired Outcome

Help participants identify the specific cue or situation that triggers the unwanted behavior (e.g., anxiety before public speaking) and decide on a positive replacement behavior or state (e.g., calm confidence).

Create the Mental Images

Guide participants to visualize the unwanted behavior or thought first—this should be clear and vivid. Then, have them create a powerful, positive mental image representing their desired state. Encourage them to make the positive image big, bright, and compelling.

Introduce the Swish

Ask participants to "place" the negative image in their mind and the positive image at a distance. Then, instruct them to rapidly "swish" the positive image into focus while making the negative image smaller and fading it away into the distance.

Repeat and Reinforce

Practice the swish multiple times until the participants feel the automatic association shifting. The key is speed and repetition—the faster the mental images "switch," the more effective the technique becomes.

Integrate Physical or Emotional Triggers

Encourage participants to incorporate a physical gesture (like snapping fingers) or an emotion (like excitement) to reinforce the swish and make it easier to access the positive state in real-life situations.

Apply to Real-Life Scenarios

Help participants imagine real situations where the old trigger might occur and use the Swish Pattern to respond with the new behavior or state. This prepares them to apply the technique beyond the training room.

Encourage Regular Practice

Reinforce the importance of practicing the Swish Pattern outside of the training to strengthen neural pathways and make the new response automatic.

The Swish Pattern is a simple yet transformative method that can bring immediate changes in behavior and mindset.

Identify a specific behavior or habit you want to develop or refine

Focus on gradual progress, rather than immediate perfection

Acknowledge and reward smallest steps toward the desired behavior

Tailor your approach based on what works best to encourage consistency and progress

Keep practicing and reinforcing until the behavior becomes natural and habitual

tête-à-tête

These techniques are like tools for your mind, and they work for anyone who wants to learn them.

*C*hoti: *Dr. Annepaul, I heard you talking about some cool brain tricks with big names. What's "Belief Change" and all the rest? Can kids do them too?*

Dr. Annepaul: *Oh, Choti! These techniques are like tools for your mind, and they work for anyone who wants to learn them. Let's talk about them one by one. First up, Belief Change. Imagine you believe, "I'm not good at drawing." Now, what if I asked you to think of three times when you made something awesome? Slowly, your brain learns that the old belief isn't true!*

Choti: *So I can change what I believe about myself? Like magic?*

Dr. Annepaul: *Exactly! Next is Reframing. It's about finding a new way to look at something. If you forget your lunchbox at school, instead of feeling bad, you can say, "That's okay, maybe I'll get to share my friend's tasty food."*

Choti: Turning bad stuff into good stuff—I like that! What's Anchoring?

Dr. Annepaul: That's when you connect a positive feeling to a physical action. For example, every time you feel super happy, you could touch your wrist gently. Later, touching your wrist brings back that happy feeling. It's your happiness button.

Choti: Ooh, I want a happiness button! What about that long one—Neuro Associative Conditioning?

Dr. Annepaul: (laughs) It sounds fancy, doesn't it? It's about associating actions with feelings to make new habits. If you want to feel motivated for homework, you could play an upbeat song every time you sit down to study. Soon, the song helps you feel motivated automatically.

Choti: That's so smart! What's Disassociation?

Dr. Annepaul: That's a clever trick to handle unpleasant memories or feelings. If something scares you, imagine you're watching it like a movie instead of being part of it. This helps you feel more detached and calm.

Choti: Like stepping outside of the problem? Cool! What's the last one—the Swish Pattern?

Dr. Annepaul: This one is fun! If there's something you want to change—like biting your nails—you imagine the old habit disappearing, and then you picture yourself doing something better, like playing with a stress ball. You "swish" away the old habit and replace it with a new one!

Choti: That sounds like magic tricks for my brain! Can we try one together?

Dr. Annepaul: Of course, Choti! Which one do you want to start with? Maybe anchoring for a happiness button or reframing to see the bright side of things?

Choti: Happiness button sounds awesome! Let's make one!

Dr. Annepaul: You've got it, Choti.

VII

Seven Habits of Effective Trainers

The 7 Habits of Highly Effective People" by Stephen R. Covey is a well-known self-help book that outlines seven principles for personal and professional effectiveness. This chapter is inspired by those 7 Habits which a trainer can benefit from if wants to be effective as a Trainer.

HABIT 1 : Be Proactive

As per Stephen Covey,

The Principle of Choice

Habit 1: Be Proactive is about taking responsibility for our lives. This is the first habit because every other habit depends on our ability to act proactively rather than reactively—to make things happen rather than waiting for them to happen. One of the key ideas in this habit is that we have the freedom to choose our response.

When things happen to us, we get to decide whether to focus on what we can change or to get stuck waiting, complaining, and worrying. One of the most important indicators of whether we're responding proactively or reactively is the language we use.

When we use proactive language, we say things like "I can" or "I get to". When we use reactive language, we say things like "I can't" or "I have to". When we use consistent, proactive language, it affirms our capacity to choose and reflects and reinforces a proactive approach to life.

A trainer can apply Habit 1: Be Proactive in several impactful ways:

Taking Initiative: Proactive trainers don't wait for problems to arise; they anticipate challenges and prepare solutions in advance. This might involve creating contingency plans for different training scenarios or continuously updating their knowledge and skills.

Positive Language: Using proactive language sets a positive tone for the training environment. Instead of saying, "We can't cover this topic because of time constraints," a proactive trainer might say, "Let's focus on the most critical aspects of this topic given our time."

Empowering Participants: Encourage trainees to take responsibility for their learning. This can be done by setting clear expectations, providing resources, and fostering an environment where participants feel comfortable asking questions and seeking help.

Focus on Influence: Trainers can focus on what they can control, such as their teaching methods, materials, and the learning environment, rather than external factors like participants' prior knowledge or attitudes.

Modelling Behaviour: By demonstrating proactive behaviour, trainers can inspire their participants to adopt a similar approach. This includes being punctual, prepared, and adaptable to changes.

Feedback and Improvement: Proactively seek feedback from participants and use it to improve future training sessions. This shows a commitment to continuous improvement and responsiveness to participants' needs.

By incorporating these proactive strategies, trainers can create a more effective, engaging, and responsive learning experience for their participants.

How do you plan to incorporate these principles into your trainings?

HABIT 2 : Begin with the End in Mind

A s per Stephen Covey,

The Principle of Purpose

Habit 2: Begin With the End in Mind is about having a plan. If we don't make a conscious effort to visualize who we are and what we want in life, then we empower other people and circumstances to shape us instead. This habit is about identifying where we want to go and who we want to be. It means defining the personal, moral, and ethical guidelines that represent the life we want to live.

One of the best ways to incorporate Habit 2: Begin With the End in Mind into our lives is to develop a Personal Mission Statement. It's like writing our own personal constitution. It reaffirms who we are, puts our goals in focus, and move our ideas into the real world.

Achieving Personal Vision

Align Actions

Ensure daily actions are consistent with your vision.

Define Guidelines

Establish personal, moral, and ethical frameworks.

Identify Goals

Recognize and articulate your life objectives.

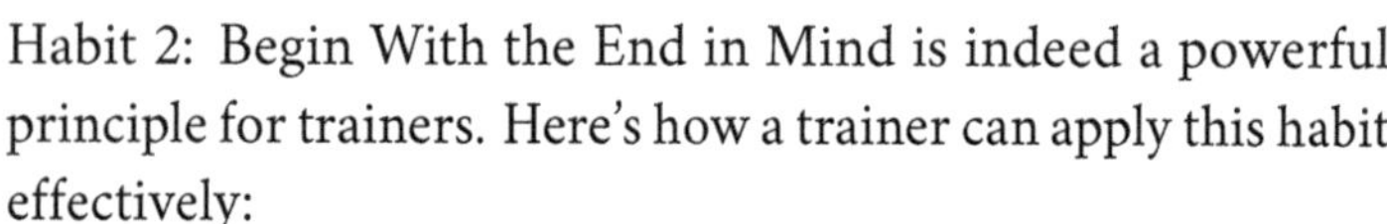

Habit 2: Begin With the End in Mind is indeed a powerful principle for trainers. Here's how a trainer can apply this habit effectively:

Define Training Objectives: Clearly outline what you want participants to achieve by the end of the training session. This includes specific skills, knowledge, and attitudes they should acquire.

Create a Training Plan: Develop a detailed plan that includes the structure, content, and methods you will use to achieve the training objectives. This ensures that every activity and discussion is purposeful and aligned with the end goals.

Develop a Personal Mission Statement: As a trainer, having a personal mission statement can guide your approach to training. It can include your values, goals, and the impact you want to have on your participants. This helps you stay focused and motivated.

Visualize Success: Regularly visualize the successful outcomes of your training sessions. Imagine participants engaging, learning, and applying what they've learnt. This positive visualization can help you stay committed and enthusiastic.

Feedback and Reflection: After each training session, reflect on what went well and what could be improved. Seek feedback from participants to understand if the training objectives were met and how you can enhance future sessions.

Ethical and Moral Guidelines: Ensure that your training methods and content align with ethical and moral standards. This builds trust and respect with your participants and reinforces the integrity of your training.

By incorporating these strategies, trainers can create a focused, effective, and impactful training experience.

How do you plan to incorporate these principles into your trainings?

HABIT 3 : Put First Things First

As per Stephen Covey,

The Principle of Focus

Habit 3: Put First Things First is about protecting time for what's most important to us. Habit 1 focuses our effort on what we can influence. Habit 2 aims us in the right direction. Habit 3 is the day-in, day-out, moment-by-moment work that takes us to that vision.

It's common to think that managing our time is about managing the clock, but it's really about managing the compass. Our personal mission is true north.

Every decision we make about how to spend our time should be orientated toward what's most important. That means carefully assessing our roles and goals and protecting time for the Big Rocks every week so they don't get overwhelmed by all the other things fighting for our attention.

Principle of Focus

Focus
Concentrating on a specific task or goal

Elimination of Distractions
Removing obstacles to maintain focus

Prioritization of Efforts
Ranking tasks by importance

Habit 3: Put First Things First, it is crucial for trainers to ensure they focus on what truly matters. Here's how a trainer can apply this habit effectively:

Prioritize Training Goals: Identify the most important objectives for each training session. Focus on the key outcomes you want participants to achieve and allocate time accordingly.

Time Management: Schedule your training sessions and activities based on their importance. Use tools like calendars and to-do lists to ensure you dedicate sufficient time to high-priority tasks.

Big Rocks: Determine the "Big Rocks" in your training—these are the essential topics, skills, and activities that must be covered. Protect time for these critical elements and ensure they are not overshadowed by less important tasks.

Role Assessment: Regularly assess your roles as a trainer. Understand your responsibilities and how they align with your personal mission and training goals. This helps you stay focused on what's most important.

Delegation: Delegate tasks that are less critical to others if possible. This allows you to concentrate on high-impact activities that directly contribute to your training objectives.

Reflection and Adjustment: At the end of each week, reflect on how you spent your time. Adjust your schedule and priorities as needed to ensure you are consistently focusing on what's most important.

By applying these strategies, trainers can create a structured and effective approach to their training sessions, ensuring they stay aligned with their goals and mission.

How do you plan to incorporate these principles into your trainings?

HABIT 4: Think Win-Win

A**s per Stephen Covey,**

The Principle of Abundance

Habit 4: Think Win-Win isn't just about being nice. It's a character-based code for human interaction and collaboration.

Most of us learn to base our self-worth on comparison and competition. We think about succeeding in terms of someone else failing—if I win, they lose; or if they win, I lose. Life becomes a zero-sum game. We start to believe there's only so much to go around, and if they get a big piece, there's less for me; it's not fair, and I'm going to do everything I can to get my share.

These paradigms of scarcity are worth shifting. Win-win is about constantly seeking mutual benefit in all human interactions—about finding solutions that are truly beneficial and satisfying for everyone involved. To go for win-win, we not only have to be emphatic, but we also have to be confident. We not only have to be considerate and sensitive; we also have to be brave.

That balance between courage and consideration is the essence of real maturity and is fundamental to a win-win approach to life.

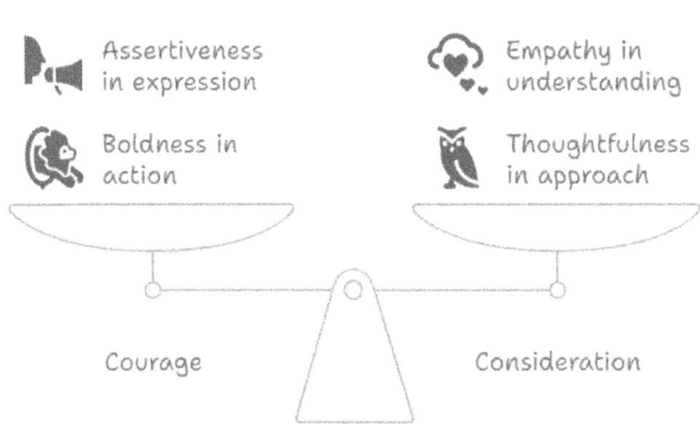

Habit 4: Think Win-Win from Stephen Covey's "The 7 Habits of Highly Effective People" very well! This habit is indeed about fostering a mindset of mutual benefit and collaboration.

Here's how a trainer can apply Habit 4 in their role:

Collaborative Environment: Foster a training environment where participants feel valued and heard. Encourage open dialogue and collaboration, ensuring everyone's ideas and contributions are respected.

Mutual Goals: Set training objectives that benefit both the trainer and the participants. For example, aim for participants to gain valuable skills while also achieving high engagement and satisfaction levels.

Conflict Resolution: When conflicts arise, approach them with a win-win mindset. Seek solutions that address the concerns of all parties involved, ensuring that everyone feels their needs are met.

Empathy and Confidence: Balance empathy with confidence. Understand participants' perspectives and needs while confidently guiding the training process. This balance helps in creating a supportive yet effective learning environment.

Encourage Teamwork: Design activities and exercises that require teamwork and collaboration. This helps participants experience the benefits of working together towards common goals.

Feedback and Improvement: Use feedback as a tool for mutual growth. Encourage participants to provide constructive feedback and use it to improve your training methods, showing that you value their input and are committed to mutual success.

By applying these strategies, trainers can create a positive and productive learning environment that benefits everyone involved.

How do you plan to incorporate these principles into your trainings?

HABIT 5 : Seek First to Understand, Then to Be Understood

As per Stephen Covey,

The Principle of Respect

Habit 5: We spend years learning how to read, write, and speak. But what about listening? What training do we get that enables us to listen so we really, deeply understand others? Habit 5: Seek First to Understand, Then to Be Understood is about listening before we speak.

Our default tendency is to try to get our point across. In doing so, we may ignore the other person completely, pretend that we're listening, or focus on the words and miss the meaning. At work, that means we might not fully understand a problem before we go to solve it. At home, it might mean we miss out on a chance at deeper connection with the people who matter most.

Habit 5 is about learning to suspend our desire to respond automatically. It's about practicing a deeper and more intentional kind of listening. And then, when it is our time to be understood, it's about expressing our point of view in a clear and articulate way that keeps our audience's needs in mind.

Components of Effective Communication

Listening	Empathy	Understanding	Expressing Views	Conflict Resolution
The act of paying attention to understand others.	Understanding and sharing the feelings of others.	Grasping the perspectives and needs of others.	Sharing one's own perspectives after understanding others.	Solving disagreements through mutual understanding.

Habit 5: Seek First to Understand, Then to Be Understood perfectly! This habit emphasizes the importance of empathetic listening and clear communication.

Here's how a trainer can apply Habit 5 effectively:

Active Listening: Practice active listening during training sessions. This means fully concentrating, understanding, responding, and remembering what participants say. Show that you value their input by nodding, summarizing their points, and asking follow-up questions.

Empathy: Understand participants' perspectives and needs before offering solutions or explanations. This helps in addressing their concerns more effectively and builds trust.

Open-Ended Questions: Use open-ended questions to encourage participants to share their thoughts and experiences. This fosters a deeper understanding of their viewpoints and challenges.

Pause Before Responding: Take a moment to reflect on what participants have said before responding. This ensures that your responses are thoughtful and relevant.

Clear Communication: When it's your turn to speak, articulate your points clearly and concisely. Ensure that your explanations are easy to understand and address the participants' needs.

Feedback Loop: Create a feedback loop where participants feel comfortable sharing their thoughts and suggestions. This continuous exchange of ideas helps in refining the training process and making it more effective.

By incorporating these strategies, trainers can create a more engaging and responsive learning environment.

How do you plan to incorporate these principles into your trainings?

HABIT 6 : Synergize

As per Stephen Covey,

The Principle of Creative Collaboration

Habit 6: Synergize is about working together to find new solutions to challenging problems. Synergy is when the sum is greater than its parts. It's often expressed as an equation where 1 + 1 = 3, 10, or 1,000. Think of the ingredients in a recipe coming together to create a dish or each instrument in an orchestra creating a song. That's synergy.

Synergy isn't an accident; it's a habit. There's a process we can follow to get there. For that process to work, we have to live all the other habits. If we're reactive, directionless, unfocused, fail to consider what others need, and don't listen to each other, we'll never collaborate successfully. We'll also never get to synergy if we don't value others' ideas.

It's truly valuing differences, instead of just tolerating them, that really drives synergy. The ideas and perspectives of others are what allow us to get outside our normal way of thinking to see the world and the problems we're trying to solve together in a new way.

Habit 6: Synergize beautifully! This habit is indeed about leveraging the power of collaboration and valuing diverse perspectives to create innovative solutions.

Here's how a trainer can apply Habit 6 effectively:

Encourage Collaboration: Design training activities that require participants to work together. Group projects, discussions, and problem-solving exercises can help foster a collaborative spirit.

Value Diversity: Emphasize the importance of diverse ideas and perspectives. Encourage participants to share their unique viewpoints and experiences, and highlight how these differences can lead to better solutions.

Create a Safe Environment: Ensure that the training environment is safe and inclusive, where everyone feels comfortable expressing their ideas without fear of judgement.

Facilitate Open Communication: Promote open and honest communication among participants. Use techniques like brainstorming sessions and round table discussions to ensure everyone's voice is heard.

Model Synergy: Demonstrate synergistic behaviour by actively listening to participants, valuing their input, and integrating their ideas into the training process.

Celebrate Successes: Acknowledge and celebrate instances of successful collaboration and synergy. This reinforces the value of working together and motivates participants to continue seeking win-win solutions.

By incorporating these strategies, trainers can create a dynamic and innovative learning environment where synergy thrives.

How do you plan to incorporate these principles into your trainings?

HABIT 7 : Sharpen the Saw

As per Stephen Covey,

The Principle of Renewal

This habit is called Sharpen the Saw because dull or rusty tools are much less effective than clean and sharp tools. The same is true for us. This habit is about preserving and enhancing the greatest asset we have to deal with life and contribute—ourselves. It's about balancing the four dimensions of body, heart, mind, and spirit.

As we spend time on each of these four dimensions of self, we create growth and change in our lives. We have the energy and vitality to practice the other six habits. We increase our capacity to produce results and handle the challenges around us.

Without spending regular time on renewal, we'll quickly find ourselves on the path to burnout and exhaustion.

The Cycle of Holistic Balance

Habit 7: Sharpen the Saw perfectly! This habit emphasizes the importance of self-renewal and maintaining balance in our lives.

Here's how a trainer can apply Habit 7 effectively:

Physical Renewal (Body): Maintain physical health through regular exercise, a balanced diet, and adequate rest. This ensures you have the energy and stamina to conduct effective training sessions.

Emotional Renewal (Heart): Foster positive relationships with participants and colleagues. Practice empathy, active listening, and effective communication to build strong connections and a supportive training environment.

Mental Renewal (Mind): Continuously seek new knowledge and skills related to your field. Attend workshops, read relevant literature, and stay updated with the latest trends and best practices in training.

Spiritual Renewal (Spirit): Reflect on your personal mission and values. Engage in activities that provide a sense of purpose and fulfilment, such as meditation, volunteering, or spending time in nature.

Balanced Approach: Integrate these renewal activities into your daily routine. Schedule time for physical exercise, mental stimulation, emotional connections, and spiritual reflection to maintain a balanced and fulfilling life.

Modelling Renewal: Demonstrate the importance of self-renewal to your participants. Share your experiences and encourage them to adopt similar practices to enhance their well-being and effectiveness.

By incorporating these strategies, trainers can maintain their vitality and effectiveness, ensuring they are always at their best for their participants.

How do you plan to incorporate these principles into your trainings?

tête-à-tête

Trainers never stop learning. They keep improving their skills to become better, just like you practice drawing to get better at it.

Choti: *Dr. Annepaul, why do you always talk about being "effective"? Is it like being a superhero or something?*

Dr. Annepaul: (chuckles) In a way, Choti, it is! Being effective means using your strengths and actions to make the biggest positive difference. It's like a superhero trainer who helps others learn and grow.

Choti: So, trainers need to be superheroes? What's their superpowers then?

Dr. Annepaul: Oh, they have quite a few! You know Stephen Covey's 7 Habits of Highly Effective People, right? Trainers can use those habits as their special tools. Want me to tell you about them?

Choti: Yes! But in a fun way, okay?

Dr. Annepaul: Deal! Habit 1 is Be Proactive. Imagine a trainer always ready with a plan, like how you pack your school bag the night before. They don't wait for things to go wrong; they make things happen.

Choti: So, they don't panic like me when I forget my homework?

Dr. Annepaul: Exactly! Then there's Habit 2: Begin With the End in Mind. This is like drawing a treasure map before starting your adventure. Trainers think about the goal—what they want their students to learn—and plan how to get there.

Choti: I love treasure maps! What's next?

Dr. Annepaul: Habit 3: Put First Things First. It's about doing the most important things first, like finishing your homework before you play.

Choti: Hmm... my mom says that all the time!

Dr. Annepaul: Moms are very wise. Habit 4 is Think Win-Win. Trainers make sure everyone feels happy and successful, like sharing candies with friends so everyone gets a treat.

Choti: Oh, I like that! What about Habit 5?

Dr. Annepaul: Seek First to Understand, Then to Be Understood. This one's special—trainers listen carefully to what their students need before they start teaching. Just like when you listen to your friend before giving advice.

Choti: I'm good at listening! What's Habit 6?

Dr. Annepaul: That's Synergize. It's about teamwork! Trainers encourage everyone to share ideas and work together, like when you and your classmates build something amazing in art class.

Choti: Teamwork makes the dream work, right?

Dr. Annepaul: That's exactly it! And lastly, Habit 7: Sharpen the Saw. Trainers never stop learning. They keep improving their skills to become better, just like you practice drawing to get better at it.

Choti: Wow, being an effective trainer does sound like being a superhero! Do you use these habits, Dr. Annepaul?

Dr. Annepaul: (smiling) I try my best, Choti. But you know, even superheroes learn from their mistakes and keep improving. Just like you!

Choti: I think I'll try being proactive, like packing my bag tonight. Maybe I'll be a superhero trainer one day too!

Dr. Annepaul: That's the spirit, Choti. One proactive step at a time, and you'll be unstoppable!

VIII

Eight Wastes to LEAN

This chapter is inspired by the 8 common wastes in operational processes, which I learned during my course on Operational Excellence for Leaders at the Indian School of Business, Hyderabad.
I have applied this learning and connected it to how the 8 common wastes that can be applied to trainers to create efficient and effective training.
I learned this technique with the word TIMWOODS. Let us elaborate on on each word in the chapters to come.

TRANSPORTATION

T ransportation in the context of Operational Excellence,

Definition:

Unnecessary movement of materials, products, or information between locations, which does not add value.

Examples:

- Moving raw materials, parts, or finished goods across long distances unnecessarily.
- Transferring documents or digital files through excessive email chains.
- Shipping products between warehouses before reaching customers.

Impact:

- Increases lead time.
- Adds handling costs and risk of damage.
- Creates inefficiencies in production and supply chain.

Solution:

- Optimize facility layouts to reduce movement.
- Use local suppliers or distribute production closer to demand areas.
- Implement digital workflows to streamline communication.

Transportation in the context of Training,

⬤ Waste:

- Sending employees to offsite training when it could be done virtually.
- Requiring trainers or trainees to move between multiple locations unnecessarily.
- Excessive back-and-forth communication to schedule or manage training.

✔ Solution:

- Use virtual training platforms (e.g., Zoom, LMS systems) to minimize physical travel.
- Centralize training materials in a digital repository.
- Automate training scheduling and communication.

Let's dive deeper into how trainers can minimize unnecessary movement of training materials and resources to achieve operational excellence:

1. **Checklist Creation**: Develop a comprehensive checklist of all materials needed for each training session. This ensures nothing is forgotten.
2. **Early Setup**: Arrive early to set up the training room. This allows time to address any unexpected issues.
3. **Strategic Placement**: Place materials in easily accessible locations to reduce the need for trainers and learners to move around.
4. **Room Design**: Arrange seating and tables to facilitate easy movement and interaction without causing disruptions.
5. **E-Learning Platforms**: Use online platforms to distribute materials. This reduces the need for physical copies and allows learners to access resources from their devices.
6. **Interactive Tools**: Incorporate digital tools like tablets or interactive whiteboards to streamline the training process.
7. **Orientation**: Begin each session with a brief orientation, explaining where materials are located and how to use them.
8. **Backup Supplies**: Keep a small stock of essential materials in the training room to handle any last-minute needs.

INVENTORY

Inventory in the context of Operational Excellence,

Definition:

Excess raw materials, work-in-progress (WIP), or finished goods that exceed customer demand.

Examples:

- Overstocking raw materials due to poor forecasting.
- Holding too many finished products that may become obsolete.
- Large batches of unfinished work waiting for the next process.

Impact:

- Ties up capital and increases storage costs.
- Risks spoilage, damage, or obsolescence.
- Can hide underlying production inefficiencies.

Solution:

- Implement Just-In-Time (JIT) inventory management.
- Improve demand forecasting.
- Reduce batch sizes and focus on continuous flow.

Inventory in the context of Training,

⬤ Waste:

- Too many printed manuals or outdated training materials.
- Overloading employees with unnecessary or irrelevant training.
- Maintaining a backlog of unused or outdated courses.

✔ Solution:

- Digitize training materials to reduce physical storage.
- Implement a "just-in-time" training approach—only provide learning when needed.
- Regularly review and update training content to ensure relevance.

Avoid overstocking training materials that may become outdated or irrelevant. Keep training content up-to-date and relevant to the current needs of the trainees. For example, ensure that all necessary materials are up to date.

1. **Scheduled Audits**: Conduct regular audits of training materials to ensure they are current and relevant. Set a schedule for these reviews, such as quarterly or biannually.
2. **Feedback Integration**: Use feedback from trainees and trainers to identify outdated content and areas needing updates.
3. **Cloud Storage**: Store training materials in a cloud-based system. This allows for easy updates and ensures everyone has access to the latest versions.
4. **Version Control**: Implement version control to track changes and ensure that only the most recent materials are used.
5. **Flexible Modules**: Create modular training content that can be easily updated or replaced without overhauling the entire curriculum.
6. **Reusable Components**: Design materials that can be reused across different training sessions, reducing the need for new materials each time.
7. **Print on Demand**: Use print-on-demand services for physical materials to avoid overproduction.
8. **Team Coordination**: Work closely with other trainers and administrative staff to ensure everyone is aware of the latest materials and updates.

MOTION

M otion in the context of Operational Excellence,
Definition:

Unnecessary movement by people that does not add value to the product or service.

Examples:

- Employees walking long distances to retrieve tools or materials.
- Poor workstation layout requiring excessive reaching or bending.
- Excessive clicks or navigation in digital processes.

Impact:

- Increases fatigue and risk of injury.
- Wastes time and reduces productivity.
- Slows down the workflow.

Solution:

- Design ergonomic workstations to minimize movement.
- Use automation and digital tools to streamline workflows.
- Implement 5S (Sort, Set in Order, Shine, Standardise, Sustain) to organize workspaces.

Motion in the context of Training,

◍ Waste:

- Employees having to go to different locations for different parts of a course.
- Trainers constantly moving between rooms or sites to deliver the same session.
- Complex or inefficient learning management systems that require excessive navigation.

✔ Solution:

- Use e-learning platforms to minimize physical movement.
- Standardize training delivery to reduce the need for trainers traveling.
- Optimize LMS usability to make training access seamless.

Streamline the setup and delivery of training sessions to minimize unnecessary movements. This can include organizing the training space efficiently and using technology to facilitate smooth transitions between different parts of the training.

1. **Designated Areas**: Create designated areas for different activities (e.g., presentation area, group work area) to minimize movement during transitions.
2. **Early Preparation**: Set up the training room well in advance. Ensure all equipment is tested and materials are in place.
3. **Checklists**: Use checklists to ensure nothing is overlooked during setup.
4. **Clear Agenda**: Provide a clear agenda at the beginning of the session so learners know what to expect and can prepare accordingly.
5. **Smooth Transitions**: Plan transitions between different parts of the training to be as smooth as possible. For example, have materials for the next activity ready and easily accessible.
6. **Backup Plans**: Have backup plans for potential technical issues or material shortages to avoid disruptions.
7. **Feedback Collection**: Gather feedback from learners on the setup and delivery of the session. Use this feedback to make continuous improvements.
8. **Post-Session Review**: Conduct a review after each session to identify areas for improvement and implement changes for future sessions.

WAITING

Waiting in the context of Operational Excellence, *Definition:*

Idle time when employees, machines, or processes are waiting for the next step.

Examples:

- Workers waiting for materials, approvals, or instructions.
- Machines sitting idle due to maintenance delays.
- Software or system slowdowns causing workflow bottle-necks.

Impact:

- Reduces overall productivity.
- Increases lead times and delays deliveries.
- Causes frustration and inefficiencies.

Solution:

- Balance workloads to ensure smooth production flow.
- Use predictive maintenance to avoid machine downtime.
- Streamline approvals and decision-making processes.

Waiting in the context of Training,

◍ Waste:

- Employees waiting for scheduled training instead of learning on demand.
- Trainers waiting for approvals or resources to conduct training.
- Delayed access to training materials due to bureaucracy or outdated systems.

✔ Solution:

- Offer on-demand learning through e-learning platforms.
- Streamline approval processes for training requests.
- Ensure training resources are readily available when needed.

Minimize idle time for both trainers and trainees. Ensure that the training schedule is well-planned and that all technical equipment is functioning properly to avoid delays.

1. **Buffer Times**: Include buffer times between activities to account for any unexpected delays.
2. **Punctuality**: Encourage punctuality among trainers and trainees by clearly communicating the schedule and starting sessions on time.
3. **Equipment Check**: Conduct a thorough check of all technical equipment (e.g., projectors, microphones, computers) before the session starts.
4. **Backup Equipment**: Have backup equipment available in case of technical failures.
5. **Reminders**: Send reminders to trainees and trainers about the session schedule and any preparatory work required.
6. **Access Information**: Provide clear instructions on how to access the training materials and any online platforms being used.
7. **Engaging Activities**: Plan engaging activities that keep trainees actively involved and minimize downtime.
8. **Time Management**: Use time management techniques to keep the session on track and avoid overruns.

OVERPRODUCTION

verproduction in the context of Operational Excellence,

Definition:

Producing more than what is needed by the customer or producing too soon.

Examples:

- Printing excessive documents that go unused.
- Manufacturing excess inventory that may not sell.
- Overproducing software features that users don't need.

Impact:

- Wastes materials, labor, and energy.
- Leads to excess inventory and increased storage costs.
- Can mask defects or inefficiencies in the process.

Solution:

- Produce based on actual customer demand (pull system).
- Use lean production techniques like Kanban to regulate flow.
- Implement make-to-order instead of make-to-stock strategies.

Overproduction in the context of Training,

◉ Waste:

- Conducting extensive training sessions that employees do not fully utilize.
- Training employees on skills they won't need for months or at all.
- Requiring excessive certifications for simple tasks.

✅ Solution:

- Implement modular, need-based training (microlearning).
- Align training content with job role requirements.
- Offer refresher courses instead of long, one-time sessions.

Tailor training content to the specific needs of the audience. Avoid providing excessive information that may overwhelm trainees. Focus on delivering concise and relevant content.

1. **Core Objectives**: Identify the core objectives of the training session and focus on delivering content that directly supports these goals.

2. **Contextual Relevance**: Use examples and case studies that are relevant to the learners' work environment and experiences. This makes the content more relatable and easier to understand.

3. **Interactive Activities**: Incorporate interactive activities such as group discussions, role-playing, and hands-on exercises to keep trainees engaged and reinforce learning.

4. **Feedback Mechanisms**: Use quizzes, polls, and feedback forms to gauge understanding and adjust the content as needed.

5. **Iterative Updates**: Regularly update the training content based on feedback and changing needs. This ensures that the material remains relevant and effective.

6. **Pilot Testing**: Conduct pilot sessions with a small group to test the content and make necessary adjustments before rolling it out to a larger audience.

7. **Simplified Language**: Use clear and simple language to explain concepts. Avoid jargon and technical terms unless they are essential and well-understood by the audience.

8. **Visual Aids**: Use visual aids such as charts, diagrams, and videos to complement the verbal content and enhance understanding.

OVERPROCESSING

Overprocessing, in the context of Operational Excellence, by definition, is performing extra work that does not add value from the customer's perspective.

Examples:

- Applying excessive polishing or painting beyond what's necessary.
- Using high-precision machining where a simpler process would suffice.
- Re-entering the same data into multiple systems.

Impact:

- Increases costs and production time.
- Wastes resources and effort.
- Can result in unnecessary complexity.

Solution:

- Standardize processes to focus only on value-adding activities.
- Use automation to eliminate redundant steps.
- Apply Six Sigma techniques to optimize workflows.

Overprocessing in the context of Training,

◉ **Waste:**

- Overcomplicated training materials with excessive detail.
- Repeating information that employees already know.
- Requiring unnecessary training sessions for experienced staff.

✓ **Solution:**

- Simplify training content and focus on core learning objectives.
- Use pre-assessments to skip redundant training for experienced employees.
- Implement self-paced learning to allow customization.

Simplify training materials and methods to focus on key learning objectives. Avoid adding unnecessary complexity to the training process that does not add value.

1. **Prioritize Content**: Prioritize content that directly supports these objectives and eliminate any information that does not add value.

2. **Interactive Techniques**: Use interactive techniques such as group discussions, hands-on activities, and real-life scenarios to engage trainees and reinforce key concepts.

3. **Step-by-Step Instructions**: Provide step-by-step instructions for activities and exercises to ensure clarity and ease of understanding.

4. **Consistent Format**: Maintain a consistent format for training materials and presentations to create a cohesive and easy-to-follow learning experience.

5. **Real-World Examples**: Use real-world examples and case studies that are relevant to the trainees' work environment. This helps trainees see the practical applications of the training content.

6. **Hands-On Practice**: Incorporate hands-on practice and simulations to allow trainees to apply what they have learnt in a controlled environment.

7. **Iterative Updates**: Regularly review and update training materials to ensure they remain relevant and aligned with the key learning objectives.

8. **Focus on Essentials**: Focus on the essential information and skills that trainees need to achieve the learning objectives.

DEFECTS

D efects in the context of Operational Excellence, by definition is the Errors, mistakes, or defective products that require rework or scrapping.

Examples:

- Manufacturing defects requiring repairs.
- Incorrect data entry leading to reprocessing orders.
- Poor software coding leading to bugs and fixes.

Impact:

- Wastes time and materials.
- Reduces customer satisfaction and increases returns.
- Can damage brand reputation.

Solution:

- Implement quality control and mistake-proofing (Poka-Yoke).
- Use root cause analysis (like 5 Whys) to prevent recurrence.

- Train employees to follow standardized work procedures.

Defects in the context of Training,

◉ **Waste:**

- Providing incorrect or outdated training information.
- Poorly structured training leading to misunderstandings.
- Employees needing retraining due to ineffective initial training.

✓ **Solution:**

- Keep training materials up to date.
- Use feedback loops to improve training effectiveness.
- Measure knowledge retention and adjust training accordingly.

Continuously improve training content and delivery methods to reduce errors and misunderstandings. Gather feedback from trainees and make necessary adjustments to enhance the quality of the training.

1. **Focus Groups**: Organize focus groups with trainees to discuss their experiences and gather detailed feedback on specific aspects of the training.
2. **Root Cause Analysis**: Perform root cause analysis on recurring issues to understand the underlying problems and address them effectively.
3. **Interactive Techniques**: Incorporate interactive techniques such as group discussions, role-playing, and hands-on activities to engage trainees and reinforce learning.
4. **Trainer Training**: Provide ongoing training and development opportunities for trainers to enhance their skills and stay updated with the latest training methodologies.
5. **Peer Reviews**: Encourage trainers to observe each other's sessions and provide constructive feedback.
6. **Pilot Testing**: Test new content and delivery methods with a small group of trainees before rolling them out to a larger audience. Gather feedback and make necessary adjustments.
7. **Performance Metrics**: Use performance metrics to evaluate the effectiveness of the training. Track metrics such as trainee satisfaction, knowledge retention, and application of skills.
8. **Follow-Up Assessments**: Conduct follow-up assessments to measure the long-term impact of the training and identify areas for further improvement.

SKILLS

Skills in the context of Operational Excellence, as per definition, is the underutilization of employee skills, talents, and creativity.

Examples:

- Assigning highly skilled workers to repetitive manual tasks.
- Not involving employees in process improvement decisions.
- Failing to provide training or growth opportunities.

Impact:

- Reduces employee motivation and engagement.
- Limits innovation and continuous improvement.
- Leads to high turnover and wasted potential.

Solution:

- Empower employees to participate in problem-solving.
- Offer training programs to develop skills.
- Create a culture of continuous improvement (Kaizen).

Skills in the context of Training,

🞓 **Waste:**

- Not leveraging employees' existing skills and experience.
- Failing to develop leadership or cross-functional skills.
- Not engaging employees in the improvement of training programs.

✔ **Solution:**

- Encourage employees to mentor and train others.
- Offer career development programs tailored to individual strengths.
- Involve employees in training design and feedback.

Fully utilize the skills and expertise of trainers. Encourage active participation from trainees and leverage their experiences and knowledge to enrich the training sessions.

1. **Peer Learning**: Facilitate opportunities for trainers to learn from each other through peer reviews and collaborative training sessions.
2. **Open Dialogue**: Foster an environment where trainees feel comfortable asking questions and sharing their experiences.
3. **Experience Sharing**: Encourage trainees to share their experiences and knowledge during training sessions. This can provide valuable insights and enhance the learning experience for everyone.
4. **Collaborative Learning**: Use collaborative learning techniques such as group projects and peer teaching to leverage the collective knowledge of the trainees.
5. **Real-World Scenarios**: Incorporate real-world scenarios and case studies that are relevant to the trainees' work environment.
6. **Diverse Perspectives**: Encourage diverse perspectives and ensure that all trainees have an opportunity to contribute, leading to richer discussions.
7. **Supportive Atmosphere**: Create a supportive atmosphere where trainees feel valued and respected. This can be achieved through positive reinforcement and constructive feedback.
8. **Reflective Practice**: Encourage trainers to reflect on their training sessions and identify areas for improvement.

tête-à-tête

TIMWOODS

Choti: Dr. Annepaul, I've been thinking... if trainers are like superheroes, do they have their own way to fight waste and be super-efficient?

Dr. Annepaul: (smiling) That's an excellent question, Choti! Trainers, like superheroes, do have their tools and techniques to fight waste. One powerful method I learned is based on the 8 common wastes from operational processes. These can be remembered with the word TIMWOODS. I learnt this when I attended a course on Operational Excellence for Leaders program at ISB, Hyderabad.

Choti: TIMWOODS? That sounds like a secret code! What does it mean?

Dr. Annepaul: It's a handy way to remember the 8 types of waste. Each letter stands for something. Let me break it down for you:
   - T: Transport
   - I: Inventory
   - M: Motion

- *W: Waiting*
- *O: Overproduction*
- *O: Overprocessing*
- *D: Defects*
- *S: Skills*

Choti: Whoa! That's a lot to remember. Can you explain how trainers can fight these wastes?

Dr. Annepaul: Let's take it step by step:

1. Transport: Trainers can avoid unnecessary movement of materials, like carrying too many papers or tools. Digital resources and effective planning can minimize this waste.

2. Inventory: This happens when trainers prepare too much material that doesn't get used. Instead, they should focus on creating only what's needed for the session.

3. Motion: Unnecessary movements, like constantly walking back and forth to access tools, can waste time and energy. Trainers can organize their setup efficiently to prevent this.

Choti: Oh, like keeping your pencils and erasers close while doing homework?

Dr. Annepaul: Exactly, Choti! Now, waiting is another waste. This happens when trainees or trainers are idle due to delays. Trainers can use this time to engage the group with discussions or activities.

Choti: That sounds smart! What about the two "O's"?

Dr. Annepaul: The first O, overproduction, is creating too much content, overwhelming the trainees. The second O, Overprocessing, is doing extra work that doesn't add value—like making unnecessarily fancy slides instead of focusing on the message.

Choti: So, trainers should keep things simple and useful?

Dr. Annepaul: Exactly! Then there are defects, which are errors in materials or delivery. For trainers, this could mean unclear instructions or inaccurate content. Reviewing and preparing well can help eliminate this.

Choti: And the last one? Skills?

Dr. Annepaul: Underutilising skills happens when trainers don't fully use their own talents or those of the trainees. Encouraging creativity, participation, and leveraging everyone's strengths prevents this waste.

Choti: That's so cool, Dr. Annepaul! So trainers can be like detectives, spotting these wastes and fixing them?

Dr. Annepaul: (smiling) That's a wonderful way to think about it, Choti. By eliminating these wastes, trainers can create sessions that are efficient, engaging, and valuable for everyone.

Choti: I think TIMWOODS is my new favorite secret code! Thanks for teaching me, Dr. Annepaul. I'll try to look out for wastes in my school projects too!

Dr. Annepaul: That's the spirit, Choti! Awareness is the first step to improvement. Keep observing and learning—you're already on your way to being a leader.

References

Moden, R. (2022b, October 14). *Blank page syndrome and how to beat it I Oxford Open Learning.* Oxford Open Learning. https://www.ool.co.uk/blog/blank-page-syndrome-and-how-to-beat-it

https://www.masterclass.com/articles/writing-tips-for-overcoming-the-blank-page

Soup, G. (2023, July 16). *Blank page syndrome:* GLOBE SOUP. https://www.globesoup.net/writing-blog/blank-page-syndrome-how-to-beat-it

Official website of Tony Robbins: Personal & Business Results coach | Tony Robbins. (n.d.). https://www.tonyrobbins.com/

Peek, S. (2025, January 2). *Management Theory of Stephen Covey.* business.com. https://www.business.com/articles/management-theory-of-stephen-covey

FranklinCovey. (2025, March 25). *The 7 Habits of Highly Effective People® | FranklinCovey.* https://www.franklincovey.com/courses/the-7-habits/

The 8 wastes of lean. (n.d.). The Lean Way. https://theleanway.

net/The-8-Wastes-of-Lean?form=MG0AV3

About the Author

Dr. Annepaul Vemagiri is a captivating author whose literary works explore the profound themes of self-discovery, growth, and resilience. Her book, From END to AND: When Your THE END Becomes THE AND, inspires readers to transform life's challenges into opportunities for renewal. In Dear Daddy, Love, Choti: Living & Celebrating Vemagiri Paul Devadatham, she pens a moving tribute to her father's life and legacy, celebrating the enduring bond between a father and daughter. Additionally, her co-authored work, Knock! Knock! Who's There? Culture, redefines learning and development, positioning trainers as trailblazers of creativity and innovation. Dr. Vemagiri's writing is a beacon of inspiration, encouraging readers to embrace transformation in every aspect of life.

Also by Dr. Annepaul Vemagiri

Knock! Knock! Who's there? Culture.
The book is a perfect mix to read about culture and development.

Do you really understand culture and development?

The same question was asked to these six writers, and their answers became a book filled with insightful perspectives that will resonate with everyone.

Dive into a rich tapestry of ideas and experiences that challenge and enlighten, offering a unique lens on how culture shapes development and vice versa.

This book is a must-read for anyone looking to deepen their understanding of these intertwined concepts.

From END to AND

Explore the Wonders of my journey from END to AND.

My journey of self-discovery is not a destination but a continuous process of growth and transformation. Throughout my life, I've delved into various philosophies, traversed diverse cultures, and engaged in deep introspection. Each experience has contributed a piece to the puzzle of my identity, revealing that understanding oneself is an ever-evolving tapestry. My book shares the insights and lessons learnt along this path, encouraging readers to embrace their unique journeys with curiosity and courage. Whether through trials or triumphs, every moment is an opportunity to learn more about who we are and who we wish to become.

Dear Daddy, Love, Choti

Here's a compelling blurb for your story:

"From the streets of Kakinada to the halls of Indian Railways, the remarkable journey of Shri Paul Devadatham is one of resilience, brilliance, and unwavering faith. Born with vision in only one eye, Paul turned adversity into opportunity, honing a sharp intellect that propelled him to extraordinary success. His contributions as an Electrical Engineer, spanning over four decades, left an indelible mark on his field, earning accolades and shaping innovation. A devoted family man and a beacon of strength, humor, and integrity, Paul's legacy continues to inspire. This heartfelt tribute captures the essence of a man whose life was a testament to perseverance, dedication, and unyielding love for his family and community."